उपदेशसारः

Upadeśa-sāraḥ

The Essence of Instruction

Three Short Texts:

Śikṣāṣṭaka,
Upadeśāmṛta,
and Manaḥ-śikṣā

I0389852

The Gopīs Seaching for Kṛṣṇa in Vṛndāvana

(Freer Gallery: The Gopis Search for Krishna from a *Bhāgavata Purāṇa*, FS-7258_18, Public Domain)

उपदेशसारः

Upadeśa-sāraḥ

The Essence of Instruction:

Three Short Texts:
Śikṣāṣṭaka, Upadeśāmṛta, and Manaḥ-śikṣā

by Śrī Kṛṣṇacaitanya,
Rūpa Gosvāmin (attributed),
and Raghunāthadāsa Gosvāmin

Verse translation
with annotations
and supporting citations
by
Morris Brand
(Madanamohana Dāsa)

Edited and introduced by
Neal Delmonico (Nitaidas)

Blazing Sapphire Press
715 E. McPherson Street
Kirksville, Missouri 63501
2021

ISBN 978-1-952232-52-7

Library of Congress Control Number: 2021931895

Published by:
Blazing Sapphire Press
715 E. McPherson
Kirksville, Missouri 63501

Available at:
Nitai's Bookstore
715 E. McPherson
Kirksville, Missouri, 63501
Phone: (660) 665-0273
http://www.nitaisbookstore.com
http://www.naciketas-press.com
Email: neal@blazing-sapphire-press.com

To Ramani for all the encouragement, inspiration, and suggestions.

Contents

Introduction **vii**
Eight Verses of Instruction vii
The Nectar of Instruction xiii
Instruction to My Mind xxiii
This Translation xxviii

Śrī Caitanya: Eight Instructions **1**
Verse One: Kṛṣṇa-saṅkīrtana 1
Verse Two: The Power of the Holy Name 3
Verse Three: Humility and Tolerance 6
Verse Four: Freedom From Other Desires 7
Verse Five: A Fallen Servant 10
Verse Six: Ecstatic Manifestations 10
Verse Seven: Love-in-Separation 11
Verse Eight: Full Surrender 12

Śrī Rūpa Gosvāmin: The Ambrosia of Instruction **15**
Verse One: The Six Urges 15
Verse Two: The Six Detriments 16
Verse Three: Six Prescriptions 17
Verse Four: Six Signs of Love 18
Verse Five: Deferential Conduct 19
Verse Six: Judgmental Restraint 20
Verse Seven: Cause and Cure of Distaste 21
Verse Eight: The Essence of Instruction 22
Verse Eight: Hierarchy of Divine Abodes 24
Verse Ten: Hierarchy of *Bhaktas* 26

Verse Eleven: Rādhā's Lake 28

Raghunātha Dāsa Gosvāmī: Instructions to My Mind 31

Verse One: Extraordinary Love 31
Verse Two: Beyond Good and Evil 33
Verse Three: Enjoined or Impassioned Bhakti 35
Verse Four: The Impediments 36
Verse Five: Help from Kṛṣṇa's Companions 38
Verse Six: Avoidance of Deceit and Hypocrisy 39
Verse Seven: Overcoming the Desire for Fame 40
Verse Eight: Kṛṣṇa's Grace 42
Verse Nine: Recollections 43
Verse Ten: Rādhā's Excellence 48
Verse Eleven: The Five Nectars 49
Verse Twelve: The Singer's Benefit 50

Appendix 1: The Life of Raghunātha Dāsa Gosvāmin 53

Appendix 2: Eight Verses on Śrī Caitanya (Śrīcaitanyāṣṭaka) 57

Verse One: Kṛṣṇa's Descent as Caitanya 57
Verse Two: Caitanya's Companions 58
Verse Three: Caitanya's Appearance 58
Verse Four: Bhakti Revealed 59
Verse Five: Caitanya's Main Teaching 59
Verse Six: Caitanya in Jagannātha's Temple 60
Verse Seven: Caitanya's Ecstatic Dance 61
Verse Eight: Caitanya's Love-in-Separation 61
Verse Nine: The Effect of Reciting this Poem 62

Appendix 3: Wishing Tree of Praise of Śrī Gaurāṅga (Śrīgaurāṅga-stavakalpataru) 63

Verse One: Caitanya's Beauty 63
Verse Two: Caitanya's Ecstatic Symptoms 64
Verse Three: Caitanya's Ecstatic Dance 64
Verse Four: Caitanya's Love-in-Separation 65
Verse Five: Caitanya's Love-in-Separation (2) 66
Verse Six: Caitanya Longs For Vraja 66
Verse Seven: Caitanya Searches for Kṛṣṇa 67
Verse Eight: Caitanya Spots Govardhana 68

Introduction

The three Sanskrit texts presented here are perhaps the earliest instructional texts in the Caitanya Vaiṣṇava movement, an ecstatic religious revival movement founded by the Bengali saint known as Śrī Kṛṣṇacaitanya (1486-1533 CE). Śrī Kṛṣṇacaitanya or simply Śrī Caitanya is believed by followers to be a descent or *avatāra* of the Hindu god Kṛṣṇa himself.[1]

Eight Verses of Instruction

The first of the texts presented here is quite likely the work of Śrī Caitanya himself. It first appears in a collection of Sanskrit poetic verses, called the *Padyāvalī*, or *A Garland of Verses* by various authors expressive of the many facets of *bhakti*[2] for the god Śrī Krsna, compiled by

[1]For an account of the life of this saint and the movement he inspired see Dr. OBL Kapoor's *The Philosophy and Religion of Śrī Caitanya* or his later work *Lord Chaitanya.* An older account of Śrī Caitanya's life can be found in his classic work *Lord Gauranga, or, Salvation for All* by Shishir Kumar Ghose. Unfortunately, there has not yet been a good critical study of the Caitanya Vaiṣṇava movement to my knowledge. Perhaps the closest to date is Edward C. Dimock's translation and commentary on the *Caitanya-caritāmṛta* (*The Immortal Acts of Śrī Caitanya*) of Kṛṣṇadāsa Kavirāja. (Cambridge: Harvard University Press, 1999.)

[2]*Bhakti* is often translated in this book as "devotion." There are some inadequacies with this translation. *Bhakti* is the feminine abstract noun of the action conveyed by the Sanskrit verbal root $\sqrt{bhaj}$ which means, among its twenty different meanings: To share, distribute, divide; to resort to, betake oneself to, have recourse to; To enjoy, possess, have, suffer, experience, entertain; To wait or attend upon, serve; To adore, honor, worship (as a god), etc. These meanings center around the idea of sharing something or having a share in something. They suggest participation in an intimate relationship with another person or other persons who share themselves or what they have with each other

one of Śrī Caitanya's close followers, Rūpa Gosvāmin (1̃480-1555 CE).[3] Because Rūpa was an older contemporary of Śrī Caitanya and spent time with him several times during his life, Rūpa's identification of the the eight verses that make up Śrī Caitanya's *Śikṣāṣṭaka* (*Eight Verses of Instruction*) is quite likely reliable. It provides our only real window into the authentic teachings of Śrī Caitanya. Other works claiming to present the teachings or philosophy of Śrī Caitanya are more likely than not appropriations of the teachings of his disciples. More will be said about this later.

Śrī Caitanya's eight verses are entirely about the process of *kīrtana*, or the musically accompanied singing of special songs, songs containing Kṛṣṇa's names and/or descriptions of his actions and qualities, as well as those of his close *bhaktas*.[4] *Kīrtana* sessions often lead to the ecstatic dancing of the participants, much like one finds in other religious traditions like Sufism and Judaism. *Kīrtana* for Śrī Caitanya was a powerful way, the most powerful way, of meditating on and connecting emotionally with Śrī Kṛṣṇa. Moreover, it is something everyone can participate in without regard for social status or communal background. The eight verses of Śrī Caitanya's work chart the emotional journey of the *bhakta* from raw beginnings to its final, refined conclusion in the appearance of an unselfish and all-consuming love for and full surrender to Kṛṣṇa. It is presumed that these verses represent Śrī Caitanya's own experience on that journey.[5]

The first verse of the eight is the core or root of the other seven. It gives an overview of the whole journey of which the later verses will supply more detailed emotive descriptions. As Madanmohandas has expressed it in his rendition of the first verse:

---

out of a sense of connection with, attachment to, or love for each other. *Bhakti* is about inclusion, acceptance, and participation. While the English word devotion covers some of these meanings, *bhakti* has a semantic range that differs from and reaches beyond that of the Latinate-English word devotion which is rooted in "making a vow." *Bhakti*, at its base, is a special kind of knowledge and a deep experience of joy.

[3]The eight verses appear in Rūpa's work as verses numbered 22, 31, 32, 71, 93, 94, 324, and 337 in the edition edited by Vanamālīdāsa Śāstrī. (Vṛndāvana (U.P., India): Rāghavacaitanyadāsa, Gaurābda 474 [1959])

[4]A *bhakta* is one who has *bhakti* for Kṛṣṇa or who is pursuing or attempting to cultivate *bhakti* for Kṛṣṇa.

[5]The Caitanya tradition came to regard Śrī Caitanya not only as a descent of Śrī Kṛṣṇa himself, but also as a descent with the purpose of revealing and modeling the behavior and experience of his own *bhakta*. He is thus called the *bhaktāvatāra* (the *bhakta* descent).

Of Kṛṣṇa's name the glory I extol,
Which polishes the mirror of the soul;
Extinguishes the worldly forest fire,
Quenching the mind's insatiate desire.
As when the moon sheds cool and balmy rays,
The lily of eternal good displays
Unfurling petals and invigorates
The Wisdom-bride, whose favour generates
A swelling tide in love's unbounded sea,
Affording at each step pure ecstasy;
Th'entire self is cleansed of every stain;
(In Kṛṣṇa's name such benefits obtain.)

It is not just Kṛṣṇa's names that Śrī Caitanya extols here, but the loud musical singing of Kṛṣṇa's names. That is, in a sense, the Names engaged by people's voices and minds. From *kīrtana* of Kṛṣṇa's names the mind (*cetas*) which is compared to a mirror is cleansed allowing the practitioner of *kīrtana* to discover his or her true self reflected there. One realizes at once that one is not the mind which is created along with and fed by the body, and instead learns of one's genuine identity which is connected with Kṛṣṇa in some specific relationship. The result of this realization is the destruction of one's worldly suffering which is compared with being trapped in a forest fire. One suffers in this way through the covering of the true self and the casting of one's sense of self onto the mind and physical body along with all the body is related to in the world. One is freed from suffering when one discovers that one is separate from and independent of the body and not subject to its vicissitudes and eventual aging and death. This is the belief of followers of Śrī Caitanya as it is with all Hindus.

Instead of burning in the flames of suffering, continued *kīrtana* feels like the cooling rays of moonlight which spread over one causing the highest good or *summum bonum* to spread open its petals like a white lotus. This is Śrī Caitanya's poetic description of the descent of *bhakti* into the heart. *Bhakti* here is described in other texts as a firm feeling of attraction for Kṛṣṇa, or *Kṛṣṇa-rati*. It is the beginning of love for Kṛṣṇa. Continued *kīrtana*, now colored by the presence of *bhakti*, brings life to one's all-but-forgotten innate knowledge or wisdom, which is compared with a "wife." Here, it is suggested that living beings are permanently wed or naturally connected with knowledge, but that knowledge or awareness which is inherent in the self of the living being has become, in its mundane sojourn, withered and weak. *Kīrtana* infused with *bhakti*'s presence brings it back to life.

As a result of the reinvigoration of one's innate wisdom, continued *kīrtana* becomes experienced as an ever expanding ocean of joy. Wisdom's being compared with a wife suggests it stands for the appearance of a more advanced form of love called *preman*, divine love, pure, selfless love for Kṛṣṇa. As a result of the presence of this kind of love, one experiences *bhakti-rasa* or sacred rapture in the performance of *kīrtana*, an expanding ocean of joy. As one's love for Kṛṣṇa continues to mature and deepen each word sung or heard in *kīrtana* becomes an experience of the fullest ambrosia, a constant flow of joy in every word. Finally, Śri Caitanya describes an experience in which the whole self (*ātman*) is washed or cleansed. This presumably refers to the washing of all residual impressions (*vāsanā*) created by previous experiences undergone by the mind and body, either in this life or in previous lives. It is held in Hindu psychology that powerful experiences, both good and bad, leave impressions in the mind that must be enjoyed or suffered again in order to be dissolved. These impressions are the vehicles of *karman* or past action and are expressed as subtle desires that influence a person's actions in the current life. They are thus subtle bindings tying a person to their minds, bodies, and pasts. Being cleansed of those subtle bindings means that one is absolutely free from bondage to the mind, body, and past baggage.

Some say that at this stage in the performance of *kīrtana* one experiences the most highly valued and intense form of divine love called the "great emotion" (*mahābhāva*). There are two forms of the great emotion: developed (*rūḍha*) and highly developed (*adhirūḍha*). Developed great emotion is characterised by the presence of a subspecies of the consequents (*anubhāva*) that are symptoms of powerful inner emotions called the *sāttvikas*: *stambha* (paralysis), *pralaya* (fainting), *romāñca* (goose bumps), sveda (perspiration), *vaivarṇya* (change of color), *vepathu* (trembling), *aśru* (shedding tears), *svara-bheda* (change of voice).[6] In highly developed great emotion the same expressions as in the developed form are present, but they have become much more distinctive.[7]

---

[6]Rūpa Gosvāmin, *Ujjvala-nīlamaṇi*, 14.158-9.

[7]ibid., 14.170:

> *rūḍhoktebhyo'nubhāvebhaḥ kāmapyāptā viśiṣṭatām|*
> *yatrānubhāvā dṛśyante so'dhirūḍho nigadyate||*

It is to this level of divine love that cleansing the whole self refers.[8] As evidence for this, a verse is cited from Śrī Jīva Gosvāmin's *Gopāla-campū* (*Gopāla's Pursuits*):

> What the ear prizes as sweetness,
> the tongue as obtained from churning
> the ocean of nectar, or the
> mind as joy in a joy-drenched heart—
> is it that fresh youth who appears
> always as the two syllables
> "kṛṣ-ṇa," or as the living source
> of rays of light in color blue?
> This inference mystifies me![9]

Here washing the whole self means drenching the whole being in joy, the ears, the tongue, the mind, the heart, including, though not explicitly mentioned in the verse, the skin with goose flesh, trembling, and perspiration, the speech with stuttering and breaking of the voice, the eyes with tears, the nose with uncontrollable flow of mucus, and so forth. The entire self is awash with ecstasy.

However, Verse Eight which refers to this final and most highly valued state of divine love as experienced through and as a result of *kīrtana* says nothing about these ecstatic symptoms. Instead, it comprehends another kind of washing of the self, the washing away of all forms of self-interest:

> He may welcome me with embraces sweet,
> Or trample me, prostrated at his feet,

> That in which the same consequents
> described in the developed form
> are seen to have reached some kind of
> undefinable distinction
> then it is called highly developed.

[8]Manindrahath Guha, *Śrī Caitanya-śikṣāṣṭaka*, 11.
[9]Śrī Jīva Gosvāmin, *Gopāla-campū*, Pūrva 15.22:

> *śravyāṇāṃ svādasāraṃ śrutiranumanute yattu yadvā sudhābdhe-*
> *rmanthāllabdhaṃ rasajñā sukhahṛdijasukhaṃ cittavṛttiryadeva|*
> *kintat kṛṣṇetivarṇadvayamayamathavā kṛṣṇavarṇadyutīnā-*
> *mājīvyaḥ ko'pi śaśvatsphurati navayuvetyūhayā mohitāsmi||*

He may to me his audience deny,
Or break my heart in any other way;
He is a rogue who does whate'er he will,
Yet he alone remains my lover still.

One is reminded here of some of the teachings of the great Christian mystic Meister Eckhart (1260-1328 CE) in his *Talks of Instruction*:

> A free mind is one which is untroubled and unfettered by anything, which has not bound its best part to any particular manner of being or devotion and which does not seek its own interest in anything but is always immersed in God's most precious will, having gone out of what is its own. ...
>
> We should pray with such intensity that we want all the members of our body and all its faculties, eyes, ears, mouth, heart and all our senses to turn to this end, and we should not cease in this until we feel that we are close to being united with him who is present to us and to whom we are praying: God.[10]

This cleansing away of all self-interest and self-identifications, this submission of one's own will to Kṛṣṇa's is what is meant in this last verse. In Śrī Caitanya's view, and Eckhart's, there is no higher achievement in the cultivation of divine love. In another passage, Eckhart makes the point even clearer:

> Start with yourself therefore and take leave of yourself. Truly, if you do not depart from yourself, then wherever you take refuge, you will find obstacles and unrest, wherever it may be. Those who seek peace in external things, whether in places or devotional practices, people or works, in withdrawal from the world or poverty or self-debasement: however great these things may be or whatever their character, they are still nothing at all and cannot be the source of peace. Those who seek in this way, seek wrongly, and the further they range, the less they find what they are looking for. They proceed like someone who has lost their way: the

[10]Meister Eckhart, *Selected Writings*, trans. Oliver Davies, 5. (London: Penguin Classics, 1994)

further they go, the more lost they become. But what then should they do? First of all, they should renounce themselves, and then they will have renounced all things.[11]

Giving away things without giving away oneself is not giving away anything at all. But, giving away oneself is giving away everything:

He may welcome me with embraces sweet,
Or trample me, prostrated at his feet,
He may to me his audience deny,
Or break my heart in any other way;
He is a rogue who does whate'er he will,
Yet he alone remains my lover still.

For a *bhakta* either treatment is filled with delight. If Kṛṣṇa embraces one, it is delight. If he tramples one down, the touch of his feet gives delight. If he is absent, he is nevertheless present. And, if he breaks one's heart, well, at a certain stage of development in love for Kṛṣṇa, even great pain is experienced as delight.[12]

The Nectar of Instruction

Śrī Caitanya's follower Rūpa Gosvāmin (ca. 1480-1555 CE) distinguished himself as one of the finest poets of the Caitanya tradition and a work attributed to him, the *Upadeśāmṛta* or *Nectar of Instruction* is the second work presented here.[13] There is some doubt in my mind that this text is really by Rūpa Gosvāmin, however. It is not found in any of the standard works of Śrī Rūpa. It is not found in his *Garland of Verse*

[11]ibid., 6.

[12]See Rūpa's definition of the stage of *rāga* in his Blazing Sapphire (*Ujjvala-nīlamaṇi*), 15.126:

duḥkhamapyadhikaṃ citte sukhatvenaiva rajyate|
yatastu praṇayotkarṣātsa rāga iti kīrtyate ||

When even great pain in one's heart
appears indeed as joy because
of deep love's (*praṇaya*) refinement, it then
is proclaimed as fervent passion (*rāga*).

[13]For an account of the life of Śrī Rūpa see my essay on him entitled "The Southern Roots of Rūpa and Sanātana" at *www.academia.org*.

(*Padyāvalī*) or in the collection of his shorter works called *Garland of Praise* (*Stavamālā*) which was compiled by his nephew, Śrī Jīva, after Rūpa's passing. If anyone knew his work well, Śrī Jīva, who was both his editor and commentator, would have. Moreover, stylistically the work in many places does not match up to Rūpa's usual high level of skill in Sanskrit composition. Finally, there is a worldliness and mundaneness about some of the verses in this work that is uncharacteristic of Śrī Rūpa's other works. Take the first verse, for instance.

> The urges of speech, mind, and wrathful ire,
> The tongue, belly and the genitals dire;
> He who's not by these forceful urges hurled,
> Is worthy to instruct and teach the world.

The verb which Madanamohanadas has graciously translates as "instruct" also means to rule, command, or control from the Sanskrit verbal root $\sqrt{\text{\emph{śās}}}$. What *bhakta* would encourage others to want to rule or control the world, or even become its teacher? Sundarananda Das, in his introduction to the 1942 Gauḍīya Maṭha edition of the text, has suggested that this verse and the two following verses are similar to verses from sections on teachings found in India's great epic, the *Mahābhārata*, especially those parts in which Bhīṣma on his death-bed of arrows instructs Yuddhiṣṭhira in the details of royal conduct in ruling over nations and empires. Though world domination or even becoming a *jagad-guru* (teacher of the world) are not goals of *bhakti*, the general idea of cultivating self-control and not giving in to one's baser urges is solid advice for anyone who wants to live peacefully and productively in human society or to strive for spiritual realization. Moreover, the second verse practically repeats the instruction of the first verse, though it does connect its advice more directly to *bhakti*, making the first verse superfluous. The second verse is:

> To eat too much, to endeavor too hard,
> To speak idly, and rules to disregard—
> Keeping bad company, and thirst for joy;
> These six practices devotion destroy.

This second verse and the one following (Verse Three) are about as simple as they come: a list of six items with a passive verbal construction at the end. They hardly required much skill to compose. The third verse, however, seems grammatically flawed to me. The items listed are in the fifth case (ablative or *pañcamī vibhakti*) and yet the construction at the end is passive. One would use either the fifth case or the passive voice to make the point, but not both. It is a flawed construction and is unlikely to be the work of Śrī Rūpa. He would never make such a mistake, nor would Śrī Jīva let him.

With respect to the fourth verse Sundarananda Das points out that many say that the verse is really the composition of Viṣṇuśarman from his work the *Pañcatantra*, a collection of animal tales that teach practical wisdom. This turns out to be true. The verse does appear as verse 39 of Book Two of the *Pañcatantra* in the recension of the Jaina monk Pūrṇabhadra (dated 1199 CE).[14] Clearly then this verse is not the work of Śrī Rūpa.

The history of the publication of this work throws some light on the question of authorship. The *Upadeśāmṛta* was first published in the 19th century Vaiṣṇava journal *Sajjanatoṣaṇī* by Bhaktivinoda Ṭhākura in 1899 (vol. 9, no.11). Bhaktivinoda claims to have found a handwritten manuscript of the text with the commentary of Śrī Rādhāramaṇadāsa Gosvāmin in the library of Śrī Vanamālī Lāla Gosvāmin of the community of descendants and disciples of Gopālabhaṭṭa Gosvāmin (1500-1587 CE) in Vṛndāvana. Śrī Rādhāramaṇadāsa Gosvāmin was a tenth generation descendant of Gopīnātha Pūjāri Gosvāmin who was a direct disciple of Gopālabhaṭṭa Gosvāmin. This places him about 300 years later than Gopālabhaṭṭa who was a younger contemporary of Śrī Caitanya; let's say about 1850 CE, give or take a decade. Śrī Rādhāramaṇadāsa Gosvāmin wrote in his commentary on the first verse of the text that the text was written or "revealed" by Rūpa Gosvāmin and consists of instructions given to living beings.[15] Some suggest the word *jīva* here refers to Rūpa's nephew Śrī Jīva, but the most likely meaning is the living being who is in need of instruction in order to gain the highest goal as conceived by the Caitanya tradition.

On learning that the *Nectar of Instruction* was first published by

---

[14] *The Panchatantra: a Collection of Ancient Hindu Tales*, critically edited by Dr. Johannes Hertel, 133. Harvard Oriental Series, vol. 11. (Cambridge, Mass,: Harvard University, 1908)

[15] Rādhāramaṇadāsa Gosvāmin, *Śrī Upadeśāmṛta-prakāśikā*, on v. 1:

> *yo hi jīvopadeśastu śrīmadrūpaprakāśitaḥ |*
> *sādhakānāmupakṛtau tadvyākhyārabhyate mayā|*

Bhaktivinoda Ṭhākura, who is known to have fabricated at least three other texts,[16] I began to suspect that he may have been the real author the *Nectar*. However, Sundarananda Das tells us in his introduction that he has found copies of the text in the library of Viśvambhara Deva Gosvāmin of Gopīvallabhapura, one of the great scholars of the Caitanya Vaiṣṇava tradition of the previous generation. In addition to that, Sundarananda Das says he found hand-written copies of the text in various collections around Vraja. I found references to two manuscripts of the text in the *Catalogus Catalogorum of Bengali Manuscripts* (Volume One)[17] Now, these may be translations of the text or they may be the text itself in Bengali script. The catalog is not clear. One is listed as author unknown (University of Calcutta, Bengali Manuscript Collection #3659) and the other is identified as the work of Balarāmadāsa (Viśvabhāratī University Manuscript Collection #3151). The Vrindaban Research Institute lists several copies of the text: four manuscripts in Bengali script.[18] Another manuscript of the text in Devanagari script has been microfilmed by the same institute.[19] This manuscript is listed as from the collection of Kṛṣṇa Caitanya Bhaṭṭa of Vrindaban. All are identified as the work of Rūpa Gosvāmin.

Sundarananda Das provides information on another hand-written manuscript of the text from a standard catalog of ancient texts by Raja Rajendralal Mitra.[20] In the description of the manuscript, Mitra says it is a "work of 43 verses instructed by Śrī Rūpa Gosvāmin to Śrī Jīva Gosvāmin and called the *Upadeśāmṛta* (*Nectar of Instruction*)."[21] Sundarananda says that Mitra cites the first two verses of the manuscript, the last verse and the colophon which Sundarananda says are substantially the same as the eleven verse version he was publishing. One wonders what happened to the other 32 verses noticed by Mitra, but

[16]See Jan L. Brzezinski, "Bhaktivinoda Ṭhakur and Bipin Bihari Goswami," in the *Journal of Vaiṣṇava Studies*, vol. 23, no. 1 (Fall 2014), 137-155.

[17]Jatindra Mohan Bhattacharjee, ed., *Catalogus Catalogorum of Bengali Manuscripts* (Volume One), 19. (Calcutta: The Asiatic Society, 1978)

[18]Mss. nos. 4343 (6111), 5056-58 (5917, 5830, and 5878-B) on pages 140 and 242 in *A Catalogue of Sanskrit Manuscripts in the Vrindaban Research Institute*, part II. (Loi Bazar, Vrindaban, India: Vrindaban Research Institute, 1978)

[19]Ms. #414 on reel 31 listed in *A Catalogue of Manuscripts Microfilmed by The Vrindaban Research Institute*, 84. (Loi Bazar, Vrindaban, India: Vrindaban Research Institute, 1982)

[20]*Notices*, vol. viii, Calcutta 1886, no. 2560, p 13.

[21]From the *Prakāśaker Nivedan* (Publisher's Dedication) of Sundarananda Das's 1942 Gauḍīya Maṭha edition of the text, 1.

missing from the published text. It is a question worth pursuing. Also one wonders where Mitra got the idea that these verses were taught by Rūpa to Jīva. Is this a misinterpretation of the verse from the commentary of Rādhāramaṇa Dāsa Gosvāmin cited above, or, is this based on other evidence?

In spite of the many manuscripts that attribute the work to Śrī Rūpa, I still have my doubts about whether he wrote the text, doubts orginally based on the stylistic and grammatical clumsiness of Verse Three mentioned earlier, not to mention the fact that Verse Four is not by Rūpa at all. The inanity of Verse One should also not be overlooked. The fact that the text may not have been written by Śrī Rūpa does not mean that there are not good things in it. In Verse Five, for instance, there is a discussion of the etiquette of respect towards *bhaktas* on different levels of advancement. This suggests the development of a fairly sizable community of Caitanya Vaiṣṇava followers, sizable enough to require guidance in proper interactions between members of the community. The advice seems sound and directs *bhaktas* towards finding the most beneficial advanced bhakta to associate with while minimizing potential for offending less advanced members of the community. The style, construction, and grammar of the verse is a marked improvement over the preceding verses. On the other hand, though Rūpa was certainly someone who had lots of respect for hierarchies, I cannot imagine Rūpa being particularly concerned about this sort of thing for two reasons. Firstly, Rūpa seems generally unimpressed by status, reputation, titles or any other traits that place some *bhaktas* below or above others. The sort of mindset this verse reveals and encourages does not bespeak an especially enlightened or evolved attitude toward classism. Secondly, Rūpa and his elder brother Śrī Sanātana and nephew Śrī Jīva were among the first to settle in Vraja. They were instrumental in "discovering" the sacred sites that came to make up the sacred geography and mythology of Vraja. It is unlikely that there was a large enough community of followers of Śrī Caitanya to require the establishment of etiquette until after Rūpa and Sanātana had passed on in the middle of 16th century. Such a community had definitely developed by the start of the 17th century.

Verse Six suffers from other problems. Though ostensibly praising *bhaktas* as transcendent or not ordinary or material, it could well be used to stymie legitimate criticism of *bhaktas* who behave badly. This rather invalidates the more sober view of the Dalai Lama to the effect that a religion is deemed good if it makes its followers better people. If Caitanya Vaiṣṇavism does not make its followers better people, what good is it? Hiding under the cloak of being "extra-ordinary (*aprākṛta*)," they can do and say just about anything and not face any accountability. It appears to close the door on anyone's right to recognize genuine flaws in *bhaktas* and could be used to disregard outrageous behavior in *bhaktas*. *Bhaktas* can carry on in any way they wish, writing their actions off as expressions their "nature (*svabhāva*)," and evade any criticism that might be directed towards them as a result. I cannot see Rūpa or any spiritually evolved person accepting or promoting this view. If this were Rūpa giving this instruction, he would in effect be proclaiming his own extra-ordinary nature. This is unlike him based on what we know of his extraordinary humility.[22] In fact, Rūpa warns against behaving as if one were Kṛṣṇa or Rāma twice in his *Blazing Sapphire*.[23] This instruction also is one that could have resulted from the growth of a larger community of believer-practitioners in Vraja as well as in Bengal.

As far as I am aware, the first time the claim is clearly made that *bhaktas* are non-material (*aprākṛta*) is in the *Immortal Acts of Śrī Caitanya* (*Caitanya-caritāmṛta*) of Kṛṣṇadāsa Kavirāja (1518-1612 CE). It occurs during a conversation between Śrī Caitanya, Sanātana Gosvāmin, and Haridāsa Ṭhākura in the third section of the text. Sanātana was suffering from some sort of skin disease that made him scratch and from the wounds created by scratching pus and blood were coming out. Nevertheless, Śrī Caitanya persisted in embracing him. Sanātana wanted him to stop. Śrī Caitanya tells him that his bodily wounds are not disgusting to him, because he did not consider Sanātana's body as material. It is non-material or spiritual. He then says:

> The Lord said: "Vaiṣṇava bodies
> are never made of gross matter.
> The body of a *bhakta* is
> not material. It is made
> of consciousness and bliss.
>
> At the time of initiation
> the *bhakta* offers himself.

[22]See his declaration in the *Immortal Acts of Śrī Caitanya*: [I am of] "low birth, low association. dependent on the lowly." Kṛṣṇadāsa Kavirāja, Cc., 2.1.179.

[23]Rūpa Gosvāmin, *Blazing Sapphire* (*Ujjvala-nīlamaṇi*), 1.21 and 3.24-5.

> At that time Kṛṣṇa makes him
> the same as himself. He makes
> that body consciousness and bliss.
> With that spiritual body
> the *bhakta* worships Kṛṣṇa's feet.[24]

The scriptural support given for this claim comes from the *Bhāgavata Purāṇa.* However the verse cited does not really support the rather bold claim that a *bhakta*'s body becomes non-material. The verse is from Kṛṣṇa's teaching to his friend Uddhava which covers chapters 7-29 of the Eleventh Skandha (Book) of the Purāṇa. The verse runs as follows:

> When a mortal gives up all work,
> offering to me his self,
> it is very pleasing to me.
> Then he gains immortality
> and is fit for oneness with me.[25]

Dr. Rādhāgovinda Nātha in his commentary on this verse cites Viśvanātha Cakravartin's commentary on it in which he says that the desiderative nature of the word *vicikīrṣita*, "wish or desire to do" indicates that this becoming non-material or spiritual is just a beginning towards making the *bhakta* free of the material qualities (*guṇa*). As the *bhakta* gradually practices *bhakti* he or she will rise through the stages of development of *bhakti* such as firm conviction (*niṣṭhā*) and so forth and should eventually become fully free of materiality (*nirguṇa*).[26]

This verse is of interest because it may give us some insight into when this text was written. If this claim of non-materiality is first made by Kṛṣṇadāsa Kavirāja in his *Immortal Acts of Śrī Caitanya*, then the *Nectar of Instruction* was written after the completion of that work, which

---

[24]Kṛṣṇadāsa Kavirāja, *The Immortal Acts of Śrī Caitanya*, 3.4.183-185.
[25]Bhāg., 11.29.34:

> *martyo yadā tyaktasamastakarmā*
> *niveditātmā vicikīrṣito me|*
> *tadāmṛtatvaṃ pratipadyamāno*
> *mayātmabhūyāya ca kalpate vai||*

[26]Kṛṣṇadāsa Kavirāja, *Caitanya-caritāmṛta*, Rādhāgovinda Nātha ed. and comm., *Antya-līlā*, p 206. (Kalikātā: Sādhanā Prakāśinī, Fourth Edition)

took place around 1612 CE. This was long after Rūpa's passing (ca. 1555 CE). Rūpa could not have written it in that case. However, if this teaching was given before in one of Rūpa's other works or in the work of some other Caitanya Vaiṣṇava prior to or at the same time as Rūpa, then he could still be the author. There is still the problem of Rūpa's aversion to *bhaktas* behaving like they were equal to Kṛṣṇa.

One of the most important bits of instruction given in this collection is found in Verse Seven and has to do with the experience of recitation of the holy names of Kṛṣṇa, a practice central to the tradition. It is often experienced as a burden or a chore by those just beginning the cultivation of *bhakti* for Kṛṣṇa. The lack of "taste" for the name is aptly compared with the disease of jaundice during which sweet things like sugar are experienced as bitter. Similarly, because of ignorance, the name is not experienced as sweet and powerful in the beginning. But if one is patient and continues the practice, one gains knowledge and understanding of the nature of Kṛṣṇa and his name, and the root of the disease, ignorance, is destroyed. A folk cure for jaundice in India is to continue to eat sweet substances even though they do not taste sweet. Although eating sweets does not really cure jaundice, chanting the holy name is believed to make it sweet.

Verses Eight through Eleven bear a strong relation to Śrī Rūpa's actual teachings. Verse Eight gives about as concise a presentation of Rūpa's view of how *bhakti* is to be practiced as can be found:

His name, his beauty, and his deeds sublime,
To hear and sing of his glory divine,
And with the conscious faculty refined,
With the tongue, by degrees, to yoke the mind—
To dwell in Vraja and follow the ways
That his loving associate displays—
Thus spending all one's time in worship skilled,
The essence of all teachings is distilled.

One is to spend all one's time gradually engaging the tongue and the mind in praising and remembering Kṛṣṇa's names, beauty, deeds, while residing in Vraja and following the example of one of Kṛṣṇa's eternal companions. This is the essence of Rūpa's advice and even if this text is not really written by Rūpa this instruction definitely bears the strong imprint of some of Śrī Rūpa's views.[27]

[27] As expressed, for instance. in Rūpa's *Ocean of the Nectar of Bhakti*, verses 1.2.226-

The three following verses also bear the strong impression of Rūpa's teaching as expressed through hierarchies. In Verse Nine the hierarchy of holy abodes is given with Rādhā's pond at the apex. In Verse Ten the hierarchy of practitioners is given with Śrī Rādhikā at the top and finally Verse Eleven is praise for Śrī Rādhikā and her pond which is hard to attain by even the best, for a single dip into that pond manifests in the bather love for Kṛṣṇa.

Though it is impossible to prove conclusively that this text is not written by Śrī Rūpa, let me close this long discussion with a summary of the reasons for doubting Rūpa's authorship and suggest instead a possible alternative authorship. The first verse is possibly from the *Mahābhārata*, though I have not yet been able to locate it. It is clearly not from a *bhakti* text since it dangles world domination as a carrot to encourage self-control. The second verse may also be modeled on a verse from the *Mahābhārata* except with *bhakti* inserted. It also essentially repeats much of Verse One, except with respect to *bhakti*. In the third verse there is a grammatical irregularity that is unlikely for a careful and learned writer like Rūpa to have made. Verse Four is not the work of Rūpa at all since it comes from a much earlier work attributed to Viṣṇuśarman called the *Pañcatantra*. Rūpa does often cite verses from other sources, but he generally identifies those sources. In my view none of these verses are by Rūpa.

Verse Five introduces a hierarchical etiquette that presupposes a sizable social community which may not have existed during Rūpa's life in Vraja and, in addition, goes against Rūpa's antinomian tendencies. Rūpa, after all, was the inventor of *rāga-bhakti*, *bhakti* that is motivated by passion for or attraction to Kṛṣṇa. *Rāga-bhakti* is a more powerful and attractive alternative to *vaidhi bhakti*, the *bhakti* motivated by respect for or faith in rules. Verse Six introduces a claim about the transcendent status of the *bhakta*'s body, an idea that may also have emerged years after Rūpa's passing. The claim is that the *bhakta*'s body and mind at the time of his or her initiation (*dīkṣā*) is transmuted into spiritual substance, though it continues to look like material substance. This happens as a result of the *bhakta*'s offering of themself completely to Kṛṣṇa (*ātma-samarpaṇa*), Thus, their bodies and minds are made fit to serve and worship Kṛṣṇa who is a purely spiritual being. Consequently, a warning is issued for others not to take any visible physical or mental

---

245,295.

flaws in the *bhakta* as evidence of the *bhakta*'s being material. Such ideas have created a sense of entitlement and privilege in some *bhaktas* which is totally against a *bhakta*'s proper self-understanding and has caused them to behave inapropriately at times.

The remaining five verses bear a closer relation to Rūpa's actual teachings. This does not necessarily mean that these verses were composed by Rūpa. Another author may well have drawn these from Rūpa's other works and paraphrased them here. These last five verses are relatively simple expressions of hierarchy and stylistically do not, to my mind, seem up to Rūpa's standard of work.

If Rūpa did not write this text, who did? At our present state of knowledge it is impossible to say with any certainty who the real author may have been. But, one can conjecture that the author lived after Rūpa and even after the composition and spread of the *Caitanya-caritāmṛta* of Kṛṣṇadāsa Kavirāja (completed in or around 1612 CE). This rests on the supposition that the claim that *bhaktas* are "non-material" first appears in the Kṛṣṇadāsa Kavirāja's book. Moreover, several of the other verses seem to be addressed to a sizable Caitanya Vaiṣṇava community such as the one that existed in the 17th century. My suggestion is that the text was written anonymously by some Gosvāmin in the community of the descendants of Gopāla Bhatta Gosvamin. The only commentator on the text is from that community and most of the manuscripts of the text, except for the few found in Bengal, come from the collections of the Gosvāmins of that community.[28] As the community of Caitanya Vaiṣṇavas grew in Vrindaban and other parts of Vraja a need was perhaps felt to summarize briefly the teachings of one of the leading thinkers, teachers, and poets of the first generation. The text was thus composed and eventually a commentary was written on it. It may have been taken back to Bengal and translated into Bengali as well. The presentation of Rūpa's essential teachings is accomplished in the last five verses of the text. The rest of the verses were addressed to the community of the time, mid-17th century or even mid-18th century, such as the verses encouraging self-control, warning of various dangers, and suggesting aids to one's cultivation of *bhakti*. The verses laying out a proper etiquette between members of the community and warnings against finding fault with advanced members of the community were aimed specially at newcomers to the community and younger

[28] See the catalogs of the Vrindaban Research Institute which often list the person from whose collection a manuscript comes.

members who might look on their superiors with overly critical eyes. The encouragement offered for chanting the names of Kṛṣṇa in Verse 7 is clearly addressed to the new and inexperienced chanters of the community who naturally would have encountered difficulties in repeating the holy names in the practice of *japa* for many long hours of the day in order to keep their vows to complete large daily counts (64 rounds or more). Whoever wrote the text may have only intended to present it as the essential teachings of Śrī Rūpa, but eventually the idea arose that Śrī Rūpa wrote the text. Whoever composed text was nowhere near as good a poet or thinker as Rūpa. Overall, the text appears to be a kind of beginner's guidebook for newly arrived *bhaktas* who have come to the holy land of Vraja to live and cultivate *bhakti*.

Instruction to My Mind

Śrī Raghunātha Dāsa Gosvāmin is the author of the final text presented here *Instructions to My Mind* (*Manaḥ-śikṣā*). Raghunātha Dāsa Gosvāmin is, among the famous six Gosvāmins of Vṛndāvana, the only non-brāhmaṇa. In addition, he was the only one among them who really had extensive and intimate experience of Śrī Caitanya. The others spent relatively brief periods in Caitanya's company, six months or a year, but Raghunātha Dāsa spent sixteen years in close association with Caitanya in Purī, right up until Caitanya's disappearance. After Caitanya's departure he settled in Vṛndāvana in the company of the other Gosvāmins, especially in the company of Rūpa and Sanātana. He is thus described as a friend of Rūpa and Sanātana by one of Śrī Jīva's disciples (Kṛṣṇadāsa Adhikārin) and he was also close to Kṛṣṇadāsa Kavirāja, who is sometimes called the Seventh Gosvāmin and who was also a non-brāhmaṇa. Raghunātha's personal experience of Caitanya's life in Purī shaped much of Kṛṣṇadāsa's account of that period in the master's life.[29] A detailed account of Raghunātha Dāsa's own life is given in the Sixth Chapter of the final part (*Antya-līlā*, Final Acts) Kṛṣṇadāsa's *Immortal Acts of Śrī Caitanya*. I will only recount a few details here.

Raghunātha Dāsa was born in Saptagrāma, which at that time was one of the best ports in Eastern India. His father Govardhanadāsa and

[29] The fourteenth through the nineteenth chapters of Kṛṣṇadāsa's *Final Acts* (Part 3) are based on Raghunātha Dāsa's *Eight Verses on Śrī Caitanya* (*Śrī Caitanyāṣṭaka*) and his *Wishing Tree of Prayers to Śrī Gaurāṅga* (*Śrī Gaurāṅga-stava-kalpa-taru*)

uncle Hiraṇyadāsa were the Zamindars or rulers of Saptagrāma and were very rich.[30] They collected the taxes for the king (Nawab Husein Shah?), sent most of them to him, and kept a substantial percentage for themselves. There is some dispute among scholars as to when Raghunātha Dāsa was born. The options are: 1494 CE (Haridāsa Dāsa and Sundarānanda Vidyāvinoda), 1496 CE (Jagadbandhu Bhadra), and 1498 CE (Acyuta Caudhurī and Dīneścandra Sen). Jānā opines that Raghunātha met Caitanya in Śāntipura in 1510. If he were only twelve or fourteen at the time, he probably would not have had the daring to try to run off to Purī by himself to join Caitanya there as Kṛṣṇadāsa Kavirāja said he tried to do after that first meeting[31] He, therefore, had to have been born sometime between 1491 and 1497 CE, according to Jānā.[32]

Dr. Radhagovinda Nath presents a very different view in his commentary on Kṛṣṇadāsa Kavirāja's *Immortal Acts*. He argues on the basis of various statements in that work that Radhunātha Dāsa was born before Caitanya. For example, Kṛṣṇadāsa Kavirāja says that when another *bhakta*, Haridāsa Ṭhākura was shifting his home from the village of Veṇāpola to Śāntipura to be near Advaitācārya, he met Raghunātha Dāsa at Cāndapura as he passed through. Raghunātha Dāsa was then a student in school there at the time:

> The boy Raghunātha Dāsa
> was studying. Haridāsa
> Ṭhākura went to see him there.
> Haridāsa bestowed on him
> his grace and because of that grace,
> he was able [later] to attain
> the company of Caitanya.[33]

From Cāndapura Haridāsa Ṭhākura went to Śāntipura where he lived in a cave on the bank of the Ganges. There he and Advaitācārya worked to bring about Kṛṣṇa's descent as Caitanya:

> Ācārya resolved to make
> Kṛṣṇa descend. Putting *tulsi*

[30] Nareścandra Jānā, *Vṛndāvaner Chaya Gosvāmī*, 222.
[31] Kṛṣṇadāsa Kavirāja, *Immortal Acts of Śrī Caitanya*, 2.16.225-6.
[32] Jānā, op. cit. 223.
[33] Kṛṣṇadāsa Kavirāja, op. cit., 3.3.161-162.

> on water, he began to do
> *pūjā.* Haridās in his cave
> did *saṅkīrtan* of the Holy Name.
> That Kṛṣṇa may descend, this was
> his wish. By the *bhakti* of those two
> Caitanya did descend to earth.
> Spreading the Holy Name and Prem,
> he liberated the whole world.[34]

Thus, Raghunātha Dāsa was already a schoolboy before Śrī Caitanya's birth. Radhagovinda Nath concludes that Raghunātha Dāsa was born in around 1469-70 CE, about sixteen years before Caitanya.[35]

There is a similar disagreement among scholars about Raghunātha Dāsa's passing date. The various dates given range from 1574 to 1587 and are: 1584 CE (Dīneścandra Sen, *Chaitanya and his Companions*), 1583 CE (Satīścandra Mitra, *Sapta Gosvāmī*), 1581 CE (Pulinavihārīdāsa, *Vṛndāvana Kathā*), 1574 CE (Harilāla Chaṭṭopadhyāya, *Vaiṣṇava Itihāsa*), 1587 CE (Murārilāla Adhikāri, *Vaiṣṇava Digdarśinī*), 1582 CE (Jagadbandhu Bhadra, *Gaurapadataraṅginī*), and 1586 CE (Madhusūdana Vācaspati, *Gauḍīya Vaiṣṇava Itihāsa*). Jānā argues that he lived beyond Rūpa and Sanātana, who passed away between 1555 and 1560 CE, and points out that Raghunātha Dāsa's name is mentioned in a deed dated 1577 CE as a intermediary for Jīva Gosvāmin in the purchase of some land around Rādhākuṇḍa for forty-four rupees.[36] If Radhagovinda Natha is correct in placing Raghunātha Dāsa's birth before that of Śrī Caitanya, then he lived a very long life, over one hundred years, too long to be credible perhaps. If the others are right in placing his birth sometime in the 1490s, then he lived into his eighties and possibly nineties. In his last work, the *Dāna-keli-cintāmaṇi* (*Touch-stone of the Sport of Tax-collection*), Raghunātha Dāsa reveals that he has become blind (verse 2) and attributes his success in completing the work to the grace of the dust of Rūpa Gosvāmin's feet:

> Even though I am blind I have
> collected this jewel of the

[34]ibid., 3.3.211-13.

[35]See Kṛṣṇadāsa Kavirāja, *ŚrīŚrīCaitanya-caritāmṛta*, ed. by Dr. Radhagovinda Nath, vol. 3 (Antya-līlā), 3.6.167, pp. 285-6.

[36]Jānā, op. cit., 231. See the English translation of the deed in Jānā, 295-8.

new sport of tax-collection, born
from the conjunction of lovely
Rādhā's river, with great waves of
mirth from the *rasa* of humor,
with the ocean of the Lifter
of the Mount, by the influence
of the dust of the beautiful,
lotus-like feet of Śrī Rūpa.[37]

An even clearer picture of Raghunātha Dāsa's condition in old age is given in another work of his, the *Vrajavilāsastava* (*In Praise of the Sports of Vraja*). In the second verse he says:

Burned completely by the forest
fire of old age, bitten by
the serpent of blindness, pierced by
the arrows of dependence on
others, and surrounded by the
lions of anger and such [am I].
O Lord, Śrī Hari! So that,
disregarding all these hurdles,
I, always calm, can worship you,
kindly make me quickly imbibe
the flowing nectar of your love.[38]

Reading these verses and a few others, it seems quite possible that he did live to an extremely old age. Quite apart from that, it is a wonderful description of the challenges of growing old.

---

[37] Raghunātha Dāsa, *Touch-jewel of the Sport of Tax-collection*, 2:

uddāmanarmarasaraṅgataraṅgakānta-
rādhāsaridgiridharārṇavasaṅgamotham|
śrīrūpacārucaraṇābjarajaḥprabhāvā-
dandho'pi dānanavakelimaṇiṃ cinomi||

[38] Raghunātha Dāsa, *In Praise of the Sports of Vraja*, 2:

dagdhaṃ vārddhakavanyavahnibhiralaṃ daṣṭaṃ durāndhyāhinā
viddhaṃ māmatipāravaśyaviśikhaiḥ krodhādisiṃhairvṛtam|
svāmin premasudhādravaṃ karuṇayā drāk pāyaya śrīhare
yenaitānavadhīrya santatamahaṃ dhīro bhavataṃ bhaje||

There are a couple of other elements in Raghunātha Dāsa's relationship with Śrī Caitanya that indicate how close he was to him and how dear. A renunciant named Śaṅkarāraṇya Sarasvatī came to Śrī Caitanya in Purī from Vṛndāvana and gave him a stone from the holy Mount Govardhana (Govardhana-śilā) and a garland of *guñjā* flowers from Vṛndāvana.[39] Caitanya would wear the garland when doing his practice of remembering (*smaraṇa*) and would hold the Govardhana stone up to his eyes, his heart, his nose to smell it, and touch it to his head. He would also bathe it with his tears and say that the stone was the very body of Kṛṣṇa. He kept these two items for three years and then gave them to Raghunātha Dāsa, instructing him in how to worship the stone.[40] The practice of worshiping stones from Govardhana as Kṛṣṇa himself has become a common practice in Caitanya Vaiṣṇavism. Raghunātha Dāsa had sixteen years to observe and serve Śrī Caitanya and in addition he was blessed with these intimate gifts from his master. His experience of Śrī Caitanya was like few others' and he wrote about it deep into his old age.

Raghunātha Dāsa's works are not voluminous. He wrote a number of small works, mostly eight to twelve verse poems in praise of people and places of special meaning to him, or, as in his work translated here, giving helpful instructions to others trying to cultivate *bhakti* for Rādhā and Kṛṣṇa. These and a few other larger poems were collected together into a work called the *Stavāvalī* or *Garland of Praises.* Not included in the *Garland* are two somewhat longer poems called the *Story of the Pearl* (*Muktācarita*) and the *Touch-stone of the Tax-collection Sport* (*Dānakelicintāmaṇi*). In addition to these works Raghunātha Dāsa, as mentioned above, supplied Kṛṣṇadāsa Kavirāja with much of the material for his description of the final period of Caitanya's life in Purī in his *Immortal Acts of Śrī Caitanya.* He may have done the same for his friends, Śrī Rūpa and Śrī Sanātana.

Raghunātha Dāsa's poetry in general has a more earthy quality to it than that of other writers in the tradition, perhaps. He refers to prostitutes and tigers to symbolize false or idle talk or residing with unvirtuous people, and he talks about liberation (*mukti*) rather than about *bhakti* in Verse Four to describe pitfalls in the development of Kṛṣṇa-*bhakti.* In Verse Five, lust and envy and other such detriments to

[39]Guñjā is a small bush with reddish black berries.

[40]Kṛṣṇadāsa Kavirāja, op. cit., 3.6.281-291.

the path of *bhakti* are compared to a gang of roadside bandits who bind one around the neck with ropes (signifying vain or useless endeavors) and hang one from the nearest tree. In Verse Six he compares engaging in cheating or deceitful acts to bathing in the flowing urine of a mule. In Verse Seven the desire for fame or status is compared to a impudent woman belonging to the dog-eaters (a class of untouchables) dancing in one's heart. In this way, Raghunātha Dāsa drives home his advice to others with graphic images no doubt representing his own struggles to overcome his wealthy and sheltered past as the son of a powerful landlord in Bengal.

Since Raghunātha Dāsa was one of the few followers who had extensive, personal experience of the founder of the tradition, Śrī Caitanya, the author of the first text of instruction in this collection, it seems wise to include Raghunātha's own description of Śrī Caitanya in his work *Eight Verses on Śrī Caitanya* (*Śrī Caitanyāṣṭaka*), also known as *Eight Verses on the Son of Śacī* (*Śrī Śacīsūnvaṣṭaka*). Thus in addition to Madanmohandas' brief overview of Raghunātha's life in Appendix One of this book, a translation of his own account of Śrī Caitanya is given in Appendix Two. Hopefully, through the presentation of these works, a more complete picture will emerge of the complex character of Śrī Caitanya and the main ideals and aspirations of the tradition he founded. Since some of the most unusual experiences of Śrī Caitanya are described in Raghunātha Dāsa's *The Wishing-tree of Praise of Śrī Gaurāṅga*, that hymn has been included, as well, in Appendix Three.

This Translation

The translation into heroic couplets by Morris Brand (Madanamohana Dasa) is based on the works of other translators. Brand has drawn some of his source translations from Kuśakratha's pre-published sheets. He has used the *Stavāvalī* edited and translated by Purnaprajna Dasa[41]. For the *Bhāgavata* he has mostly used the translation of Tapasyananda Swami.[42] For the *Upadeśāmṛta* (*The Nectar of Instruction*) he has used the Bengali edition published by Keśava Gauḍīya Maṭha.[43] Finally, he has consulted various of the translations of Advaita dasa.

[41]Vrindaban: Ras Bihari Lal Sons, 2001.

[42]Chennai (Madras): Sri Ramakrishna Math, [1980], four volumes.

[43]Rūpa Gosvāmin, *Śrī Upadeśāmṛta*. (New Delhi: Śrī Gauḍīya Vedānta Samiti, 1997)

As for myself, I have generally relied on editions of the texts in the original languages (Sanskrit and Bengali). In addition to the references given in the footnotes, I have used the edition of Raghunātha Dāsa's *Stavāvalī* edited by Rāmanārāyaṇa Vidyāratna with the commentary of Baṅgeśvara Vidyābhūṣaṇa.[44] I also compared the texts of Raghunātha Dāsa Gosvāmin with those in the superb edition of his *Stavāvalī* edited by Purīdāsa.[45] For the *Eight Verses of Instruction* of Śrī Caitanya I have referred to the edition with Bengali translation and commentary of Manīndranātha Guha[46] as well as to Vanamālīdāsa Śāstrī's edition of Śrī Rūpa's *Garland of Verses* (*Padyāvalī*) with Hindi translation.[47] For the *Nectar of Instruction* (*Upadeśāmṛta*), attributed to Śrī Rūpa, I consulted the edition published by Sundaradāsa Vidyāvinoda, which is probably substantially the same as the one Brand consulted.[48] In this edition I relied on parts of the introduction by Sundarānanda and on the Sanskrit commentary by Śrī Rādhāramaṇadāsa Gosvāmin.

[44]Murśidābād: Rādhāramaṇa Press, 1329 Baṅgābda [1923] 2nd ed.

[45]Mayamanasiṃha: Śrī Śacīnārāyaṇa Caturdhurīna, 1947.

[46]Vṛndāvana: Sāvitrī Guha, [1971]

[47]Vṛndāvana: Rāghavacaitanya Dāsa, 1959.

[48]Kolkātā: Gauḍīya Maṭha, 1942. There are surprizingly several misprints in the text of this edition. This was found at www.archive.org without a proper title page.

Kṛṣṇa meeting with Rādhā

(Freer Gallery: Krishna approaches Radha, folio from a *Rasikapriyā*, FS-S2018.1.45, Public Domain)

Śrī Caitanya: Eight Instructions

Verse One: Kṛṣṇa-saṅkīrtana

The eight verses of the *Śikṣāṣṭaka*, attributed to Śrī Caitanya deva were originally included in Śrī Rūpa's anthology *Padyāvalī*, and whether they were originally conceived as a single work, or subsequently arranged into a single theme, is not clear. Aside from two or three other verses, Śrī Caitanya has not left any writings in his own hand. One reason, perhaps, for his not having written more, is that his life and conduct were themselves the very themes of poetry. Reading the accounts of his life, and noting the time he spent relishing poetry, one realizes he had no time for composition of complex narratives and philosophical tracts.

Someone might object that, aside from verse three, none of the verses of *Śikṣāṣṭaka* can be called "teachings," to which it may be replied that, indeed that is true, but they have been taken as such, insofar as they teach by example. It would seem apparent that the formulation of doctrine and narratives on Kṛṣṇa's deeds were left to his adherents and followers, many of whom were highly skilled poets and rhetors. Due to the potent influence of Śrī Caitanya there was subsequently a promiscuous bursting forth in the lush and fertile garden of poesy. In the first verse are enumerated the gradual stages of the development of *bhakti*, from the initial commencement of devotional disciplines to the attainment of ecstatic love for Kṛṣṇa.

चेतोदर्पणमार्जनं भवमहादावाग्निनिर्वापनं
श्रेयःकैरवचन्द्रिकावितरणं विद्यावधूजीवनम् ।
आनन्दाम्बुधिवर्धनं प्रतिपदं पूर्णामृतास्वादनम्
सर्वात्मस्नपनं परं विजयते श्रीकृष्णसङ्कीर्तनम् ॥ १ ॥

cetodarpaṇamārjanaṃ bhavamahādāvāgninirvāpanaṃ
śreyaḥkairavacandrikāvitaraṇaṃ vidyāvadhūjīvanam |
ānandāmbudhivardhanaṃ pratipadaṃ pūrṇāmṛtāsvādanam
sarvātmasnapanaṃ paraṃ vijayate śrīkṛṣṇasaṅkīrtanam || 1||

Of Kṛṣṇa's name the glory I extol,
Which polishes the mirror of the soul;
Extinguishes the worldly forest fire,
Quenching the mind's insatiate desire;
As when the moon sheds cool and balmy rays,
The lily of eternal good displays
Unfurling petals and invigorates
The Wisdom-bride, whose favour generates
A swelling tide in love's unbounded sea,
Affording at each step pure ecstasy;
Th'entire self is cleansed of every stain;
(In Kṛṣṇa's name such benefits obtain.)

The stages of the gradual development of ecstatic love in the aspirant are outlined by Śrī Rūpa,

First there is faith, then holy company,
Then worship practised with sincerity,
Impediments are attenuated,
Then comes relish, then addiction,
Thereon emotion rises by degrees,
To the attainment of love's ecstasies.
These stages followed by the aspirant,
Reveal of love the final fulfilment.[1]

The effects of the gradual development of ecstatic love are outlined by Śrī Rūpa,

[1]Brs., 1.4.15-16

All sore afflictions it eradicates,
And blessedness and fortune instigates;
It makes emancipation[2] trifling seem,
And is rarely attained in the extreme;
Its particular innate property
Is that of an intense felicity;
Love is of such pure happiness the cause,
Kṛṣṇa himself, attracted, to it draws.[3]

Gajendra, the elephant king, observes this about the effects of devotion,

When they about your wonderful deeds sing—
Which all auspiciousness and blessings bring—
They are submerged in the unbounded sea,
Of bliss divine and loving ecstasy.[4]

We also find in the *Viṣṇu Purāṇa* a statement on the eradication of misery and the attainment of bliss,

Attainment of the Lord is deemed to be,
By learned ones, the greatest remedy
To cure the afflictions of three-fold pain,
That in the womb, at birth, and age obtain.
It is attended by exclusive bliss,
The singular and final happiness.[5]

Verse Two: The Power of the Holy Name

A proclamation of the transcendental powers of Kṛṣṇa's various names, and an expression of humility and longing.

नाम्नामकारि बहुधा निजसर्वशक्ति-
स्तत्रार्पिता नियमितः स्मरणे न कालः ।
एतादृशी तव कृपा भगवन्ममापि

[2]Liberation from repeated birth and death.
[3]Brs., 1.1.17
[4]Bhāg., 8.3.20
[5]V.P., 6.58-9

दुर्दैवमीदृशमिहाजनि नानुरागः ॥ २ ॥

nāmnāmakāri bahudhā nijasarvaśakti-
statrārpitā niyamitaḥ smaraṇe na kālaḥ |
etādṛśī tava kṛpā bhagavanmamāpi
durdaivamīdṛśamihājani nānurāgaḥ || 2 ||

You are, O Lord, by diverse names renowned,
Each name with your own potency endowed;
You have conferred, in disinterested grace,
No rules of cleanliness or time or place,
In contemplation of your holy name;
Yet I am fraught with misery and shame;
Since in despite of your great favor shown,
No love in me for your sweet name has grown.

"Each name with you own potency endowed," implies Kṛṣṇa the person and Kṛṣṇa the name are the same, unlike the usual distinction between the person and their name.

The thought-gem of Kṛṣṇa's name is endued,
With conscious beauty and beatitude;
Complete, hallowed, free and unrestrained,
Since the name is not different from the named.[6]

Also,

Of all things sweet this is purest sweetness,
Most auspicious of all auspiciousness;
It is the choicest, ripest fruit divine,
That grows upon the holy scripture's vine.
When uttered in faith, or even in disdain,
A human being straightway does attain,
Salvation, best of Bhṛgus; I proclaim,
Such is the potency of Kṛṣṇa's name.[7]

Moreover,

---

[6] *Padma Purāṇa.* Cited in Rūpa's Brs., 1.2.233.
[7] *Padyāvalī* 26. Attributed to Veda Vyāsa.

The sacred name of Hari, Hari's name,
The name of Hari is the only gain;
Nor this, nor that, nor other means are there,
In Kali's age to bring about welfare.[8]

The superlative excellence of chanting Hari's name in this degenerate age is propounded by Śuka Muni in the *Śrīmad Bhāgavata*,

O king, this Kali age is fraught with vice,
Yet there is but one virtue will suffice:
By singing Kṛṣṇa's holy name and fame,
The soul may freedom from bondage attain.[9]

Describing the powerful effects of Kṛṣṇa's name on Rādhā, Paurṇamāsī addresses Nāndīmukhī, in Śrī Rūpa's *Vidagdha-mādhava*, Act I,

Ah me! what nectar flows, pure and refined,
When the syllables 'Kṛṣ', and 'na' are joined;
When on the tongue to dance and play it learns,
For many tongues the eager chanter yearns;
And when it gains into the ear ingress,
A million ears the chanter would possess;
But when in the heart's courtyard it alights,
It ravishes the senses with delight;
The faculties of sense are all undone,
And then the chanter falls down in a swoon.[10]

Śrī Rūpa even suggests that the name is better than the named,

O name divine, your nature is two-fold,
That which is signified, and the word told;
And there is no distinction twixt the two.
Yet of the latter we know this is true:
A more abundant mercy has been shown
Since by the word a creature may atone
For heaps of sins in endless multitude,
And plunge into the sea of beatitude.[11]

---

[8] *Bṛhan-nāradīya Purāṇa*, (?).
[9] Bhāg., 12.3.51.
[10] *Vidagdha-mādhava*, 1.15.
[11] *Nāmāṣṭaka*, 6

Verse Three: Humility and Tolerance

Developing the theme in the foregoing verse of longing and humility, the divine author prescribes the ideal disposition to be entertained by the aspirant for the practice of Hari-nāma-saṅkīrtana, ie, the singing of Kṛṣṇa's name and glory, and advises the cultivation of unassuming meekness, tolerance, humility, and respect for others,

तृणादपि सुनीचेन
तरोरिव सहिष्णुना ।
अमानिना मानदेन
कीर्तनीयः सदा हरिः ॥ ३ ॥

tṛṇādapi sunīcena
taroriva sahiṣṇunā |
amāninā mānadena
kīrtanīyaḥ sadā hariḥ || 3 ||

Endued with meek sincere humility,
More low than straw, forbearing as a tree;
Devoid of pride, still others honouring;
Thus one may Hari's name constantly sing.

Sanātana Gosvāmī, in his *Bṛhad-bhāgavatāmṛta*, defines '*dainya*' or humility,

Although endowed with rarest quality,
He deems himself as base and unworthy,
Which extraordinary state of mind,
The learned ones as 'dainya' have defined.[12]

By word and deed the wise should cultivate
Modesty and maintain a humble state,
And anything contrary to this view,
With diligence and care he will eschew.[13]

---

[12]Bba., 2.5.222.
[13]Bba., 2.5.223.

Kṛṣṇa advises Uddhava to show respect to all embodied beings,

Not caring for the mocking of his friends,
Quite unabashed, in humbleness he bends,
And prostrated upon the earth he bows,
To dogs and pariahs, asses, and cows.[14]

Nārada to the Pracetasas.

Within all bodied beings there abides
The self, wherein Lord Śrī Hari resides,
Thus in all, and everywhere try to see
The self, and you will thus please Lord Hari.[15]

On the efficacy of reciting Kṛṣṇa's names with humility and longing, there is a passage in the *Narasiṃha Purāṇa*,

Whoso, 'O Kṛṣṇa, Kṛṣṇa, Kṛṣṇa!', cries,
I raise that person as the lotus rise
Above the waters where they once did dwell,
E'en so, I lift them out of deepest hell.

And whosoever on me loudly calls,
While in prostration, on the ground he falls;
'O Lotus-eyed!, O God of gods!' I sue,
'O Lion-man! I seek refuge in you.

'O Janārdan! O you of triple stride!
'In you alone for succor I confide!'
Thus those who seek me and earnestly pray,
I elevate and drive their grief away.[16]

Verse Four: Freedom From Other Desires

Now, from text four to the end a connected theme can be observed in respect to the progress of ardent longing. The Great Master, if I may use the term for Mahāprabhu illustrates, by example, how the devotee's

[14]Bhāg., 11.29.16.
[15]Bhāg., 6.4.13.
[16]*Narasiṃha Purāṇa*, 8.27-29.

longing is intensified and augmented. In text four, presently under discussion, is seen how the votary prays for disinterested devotion to the exclusion of extraneous desires for righteousness, wealth, pleasure, and even the termination of metempsychosis.

न धनं न जनं न सुन्दरीं
कवितां वा जगदीश कामये ।
मम जन्मनि जन्मनीश्वरे
भवताद्भक्तिरहैतुकी त्वयि ॥ ४ ॥

na dhanaṃ na janaṃ na sundarīṃ
kavitāṃ vā jagadīśa kāmaye |
mama janmani janmanīśvare
bhavatādbhaktirahaitukī tvayi || 4 ||

I have no wish for wealth, friends, or commerce
With fair beauties depicted in choice verse;
But grant, O Universal Lord, to me,
From birth to birth, sans motive, love for thee.

Divine love or *bhakti* is defined by Śrī Rūpa in his *Bhakti-rasāmṛta-sindhu,*

Without extraneous aspiration,
Nor hid by pious works or abstraction;
To cultivate a pleasing attitude
For Kṛṣṇa, is the best beatitude[17]

When from all conditioning adjuncts free,
With firm dedication and purity,
When by the sense faculties is adored,
Lord Hṛṣīkeś, the sense faculties' Lord,
The definition true will thus be shown,
Of pure love, by the name of *bhakti* known.[18]

Bhakti to Puruṣottam is indeed

[17]Brs., 1.1.11.
[18]*Nārada Pañcarātra*, cited in Brs., 1.1.12.

Sans motive, and naught might it impede.[19]

E'en if I offer to my devotee,
My wealth, realm, form or close proximity,
Or even oneness, still they would not swerve
To accept these, if me they could not serve.[20]

Also there is a famous stanza by Rāma-priya Hanumān,

O you who break the bonds of existence,
In loving you I seek no recompense;
For emancipation I do not pray,
Which makes the loving bonds dissolve away,
Where I am the servant and you my Lord,
My dear and cherished master most adored.[21]

In a similar strain, the author of *Jagannāthāṣṭaka* makes his submission,

I pray not for kingdom, nor wealth, nor gem,
Nor comely wife, desired by all men;
But let me sing forever and always,
Your glory which the Lord of ghosts does praise;
And may Lord Jagannāth Swāmī alight
Within my field of vision—in my sight.[22]

In Vritra's prayer from Book Six, is illustrated the deep longing of the devotee,

E'en as the fledgling, with eagerness stirred,
Awaits the succor of the mother bird,
As thirsty calves await the mother kine,
As for her husband does the dear wife pine,
Thus even so, I yearn and long to see,
A vision, O Lotus-eyed one, of thee.[23]

---

[19] ibid., 1.1.13. Cited from second half of Bhāg. 3.29.12.
[20] ibid., 1.1.14. Cited from Bhāg., 3.29.13.
[21] Bba., 1.4.68.
[22] *Jagannāthāṣṭaka*, 7.
[23] Bhāg., 6.11.26.

Verse Five: A Fallen Servant

The devotee with a feeling of helpless insignificance, fondly entreats for the least of grace, indicating a further development in the intensity of ardent longing.

अयि नन्दतनुज किङ्करं
पतितं मां विषमे भवाम्बुधौ ।
कृपया तव पादपङ्कज-
स्थितधूलिसदृशं विचिन्तय ॥ ५ ॥

ayi nandatanuja kiṅkaraṃ
patitaṃ māṃ viṣame bhavāmbudhau |
kṛpayā tava pādapaṅkaja-
sthitadhūlisadṛśaṃ vicintaya || 5 ||

O son of Nanda! I am but thy slave
Sunk in the sea of worldliness, O save!
To save this servant would be kind and just,
If you consider me but as the dust
Or flower pollen, while I do entreat,
Adhering to the soles of thy dear feet.

The 10th century devotee/philosopher, Yāmunācārya, in his *Stotra-ratna*, addresses his supplication to Śrī Hari, for the status of eternal servitude,

I will always attend thee, devoted,
With all mental disturbance quieted,
When will I thine eternal servant be,
My Master, and afford delight to thee?[24]

Verse Six: Ecstatic Manifestations

नयणं गलदश्रुधारया
वदनं गद्गद्रुद्धया गिरा ।

[24] Yāmunācārya, *Stotra-ratna*, 46.

पुलकैर्निचितं वपुः कदा
तव नामग्रहणे भविष्यति ॥ ६ ॥

nayanaṃ galadaśrudhārayā
vadanaṃ gadgadruddhayā girā |
pulakairnicitaṃ vapuḥ kadā
tava nāmagrahaṇe bhaviṣyati || 6 ||

Ah! when will those tears stream down from my eyes,
When will my voice be choked, which speech denies,
When will the hairs rise up o'er all my frame,
As I take up the chanting of thy name?

The *Śrīmad Bhāgavata* illustrates the attainment of ecstatic emotions in the sermon of the nine yogins; the two verses cited below have been determined to be the very essence of the text.

When ears can drink the hallowed deeds of him,
Whose hands are marked by signs, the wheels of fate,
When songs his names and births and deeds relate,
When he deigns in the world to incarnate;
Then one should wander, unattached and free,
And unabashed sing loud his high glory.

Thus sworn to sing and chant the loved name,
A mind melting passion he does attain,
Now laughs, now sings, now weeps in sad despair,
Now dances like a madman without care.[25]

Verse Seven: Love-in-Separation

युगायितं निमेषेण
चक्षुषा प्रावृषायितम् ।
शून्यायितं जगत्सर्वं
गोविन्दविरहेण मे ॥ ७ ॥

[25] Bhāg., 11.2.39-40.

yugāyitaṃ nimeṣeṇa
cakṣuṣā prāvṛṣāyitam |
śūnyāyitaṃ jagatsarvaṃ
govindaviraheṇa me || 7 ||

A mere moment becomes an age of pain,
Tears fall in torrents like the monsoon rain,
A gloomy void is all the world, abhorred
In absence of Govinda, my sweet Lord!

In the anguish of impending separation, the cowherd damsels complained,

When he with ardent love and tender grace,
Sweet speech, the playful glance, the firm embrace,
Foregathered on those nights to dance the Rās,
Full many nights as one moment did pass;
How shall we endure the protracted time,
Of his desertion, but to mourn and pine?

He at day's end to Vraja would repair,
With dust upon his garland and his hair,
The dust by tramping hooves of kine upraised.
Then by his friends Ananta's friend was praised.
Moreover when he played the flute and smiled,
Our minds were captivated and beguiled.
How can we endure separation, how
Can we sustain our lives in sorrow now?[26]

Verse Eight: Full Surrender

In the concluding text of *Śikṣāṣṭaka*, Śrī Caitanya speaks in the voice of Rādhā after a fit of pride or misunderstanding or severance for some other reason.

आश्लिष्य वा पादरतं पिनष्टु माम्
अदर्सनान्मर्महतं करोतु वा ।

[26]Bhāg., 10.39.29-30.

यथा तथा वा विदधातु लम्पटो
मत्प्राणनाथस्तु स एव नापरः ॥ ८ ॥

āśliṣya vā pādaratam pinaṣṭu mām
adarsanānmarmahataṃ karotu vā |
yathā tathā vā vidadhātu lampaṭo
matprāṇanāthastu sa eva nāparaḥ || 8 ||

He may welcome me with embraces sweet,
Or trample me, prostrated at his feet,
He may to me his audience deny,
Or break my heart in any other way;
He is a rogue who does whate'er he will,
Yet he alone remains my lover still.

An illustration of Śrī Caitanya's relishing of divine poetry can be had in the *Caitanya-caritāmṛta.* In a passage where the Great Master in discussion with divine Nityānanda and others survey the life and acts of Mādhavendra Purī, they analyse one of his verses, something like this,

This stanza is so wonderful and rare,
That there is nothing with it to compare;
Just as Malaya Candan, rubbed and ground,
Spreads its sweet fragrance more and more around,
E'en so, the odour of this verse is spread,
The more it is with deep attention read.

Or, as among heaps of gems in a mine,
This verse does like the Kaustubha gem shine.
This verse of rapturous poems is the best,
By Rādhā Ṭhākurāṇī first expressed;
Then Mādhavendra, by her grace inspired,
Composed this verse in heat of fancy fired;

No fourth person beside Gaura exists,
Who of this verse can relish the sweet bliss;
And at his life's end Purī did attain,
Reciting this verse o'er and o'er again,
Beatitude, and high perfection gain.

(the verse)

O Lord whose heart melts pitying the poor!
Mathurā's Lord! will I e'er see you more?
My heart is rent with grief, not seeing you,
Ah me alas! dear Lord, what shall I do?[27]

Hearing the verse, then falling to the ground,
The Master, in love frenzy, rolled around;
Nitāi, in anxious haste, fearing mishap,
Caught hold of him and held him in his lap;
Then, after weeping much, Gaura began,
Deranged by madness, here and there to run,
In ardent ecstasy and love's sweet pang,
The Master yelled and laughed and danced and sang,
'O Lord whose heart! O Lord whose heart!' he cried.
But with emotion choked the accent died;
And lamentably Gaura wept and cried,
While tears rushed from the sluices of his eyes.[28]

---

[27] Rūpa, *Padyāvalī*, 334:

ayi dīnadayārdranātha he
mathurānātha kadāvalokyase |
hṛdayaṃ tvadālokakātaraṃ
dayita bhrāmyati kiṃ karomyaham ||

[28] Kṛṣṇadāsa Kavirāja, *Caitanya-caritāmṛta*. Madhya, 4, 192-202.

Śrī Rūpa Gosvāmin: The Ambrosia of Instruction

Verse One: The Six Urges

वाचो वेगं मनसः क्रोधवेगं
जिह्वावेगमुदरोपस्थवेगम् ।
एतान् वेगान् यो विषहेत धीरः
सर्वामपीमां पृथिवीं स शिष्यात् ॥ १ ॥

vāco vegaṃ manasaḥ krodhavegaṃ
jihvāvegamudaropasthavegam |
etān vegān yo viṣaheta dhīraḥ
sarvāmapīmāṃ pṛthivīṃ sa śiṣyāt || 1 ||

The urges of speech, mind, and wrathful ire,
The tongue, belly and the genitals dire;
He who's not by these forceful urges hurled,
Is worthy to instruct and teach the world.

According to the commentator (Rādhāramaṇa Dāsa Gosvāmin), the mind's urge is the thirst or craving for *asat* such as, say, vain and idle pursuits and fancies, which are again stirred by the senses, eyes, ears, nose, etc. He then goes on to cite a couplet from the *Padma Purāṇa*, also quoted in Rūpa's *Bhakti-rasāmṛta-sindhu*, something like this,

How can Mukunda, in a mind distressed

By misery and grief, be manifest?[1]

Interestingly, another commentator concludes by proposing that the instructions in relation to exercising control over the six mentioned urges are directed to the householder, or one who has not renounced the world, since those who have renounced the world ought to have already mastered these urges. But I don't suppose there is any harm in reminding them.

Regarding the urges or *vega*-s, Śrī Kṛṣṇa says to Arjuna,

But whoever can these urges tolerate,
While in the mortal and bodily state,
And is not by desire and wrath consumed—
He is a happy man, and well attuned.[2]

Madhusūdana Sarasvatī (circa 1650 CE), examining this verse, elaborates on the word *vega* or urges: "Their intensive states (desire and wrath) hinder the memory regarding what is opposed to custom and the Vedas, manifesting themselves in the form of one's being on the verge of acting contrary to custom and the Vedas. Therefore they are called *vega*, onrush, because of their similarity to the rush of a stream. Indeed, as the rush of a stream, becoming very strong in the rainy season, drowns by throwing into a hollow and pushing downwards even one who is unwilling ... ."[3]

Verse Two: The Six Detriments

अत्याहारः प्रयासश्च प्रजल्पो नियमाग्रहः ।
जनसङ्गश्च लौल्यं च षड्भिर्भक्तिर्विनश्यति ॥ २ ॥

atyāhāraḥ prayāsaśca prajalpo niyamāgrahaḥ |
janasaṅgaśca laulyaṃ ca ṣaḍbhirbhaktirvinaśyati || 2 ||

[1]Brs., 1.2.115:

śokāmarṣādibhirbhāvairākrāntaṃ yasya mānasam |
kathaṃ tasya mukundasya sphūrtisambhāvanā bhavet ||

[2]*Bhagavad-gītā*, 5.23
[3]Swami Gambhirananda trans.

To eat too much, to endeavor too hard,
To speak idly, and rules to disregard—
Keeping bad company, and thirst for joy;
These six practices devotion destroy.

The second verse proposes six detriments to devotional disciplines, *atyāhāra*—overeating, *prayāsa*—over endeavour, *prajalpa*—idle speech, *niyamāgraha*—disregard of rules, which can also read as over zealous adherence to rules; *janasaṅga*—worldly association(s); and *laulya*—hankering or inconstancy. In reference to things detrimental, a verse is cited defining the six signs of the progress of self surrender,

Acceptance of those things favourable,
And forsaking the unfavourable;
Confidence in protective care divine;
The care of one's maintenance to resign;
The soul, in self surrender to consign;
An unassuming temperament and meek,
These are six signs of those who refuge seek.[4]

Verse Three: Six Prescriptions

उत्साहान्निश्चयाद्धैर्यात्तत्तत्कर्मप्रवर्तनात् ।
सङ्गत्यागात्सतो वृत्तेः षड्भिर्भक्तिः प्रसिध्यति ॥ ३ ॥

utsāhānniścayāddhairyāttattatkarmapravartanāt |
saṅgatyāgātsato vṛtteḥ ṣaḍbhirbhaktiḥ prasidhyati || *3* ||

Zeal and conviction and firm endurance,
The practice of devout deeds to commence;
Eschewing attachment and company
To cultivate holy society;

[4]A Vaiṣṇava tantra:

ānukūlyasya saṅkalpaḥ prātikūlyasya varjanam |
rakṣiṣyatīti viśvāso goptṛtve varaṇaṃ tathā |
ātmanikṣepa-kārpaṇye ṣaḍvidhā śaraṇāgatiḥ ||

These six articles of faith, when pursued,
Grant devotion's perfect beatitude.

Having dealt with the impediments and detriments in the first two verses, the author proceeds to enumerate positive prescriptions. In the first two lines are illustrated the disposition for the cultivation of those acts that nourish (advance) devotional sentiments. The next two lines indicate the outward conduct which assists in the avoidance of impediments and adherence to a congenial discipline. *Utsāha*—zeal, eager enthusiasm; *niścaya*—unwavering conviction; *dhairya*—steadiness, endurance and sobriety.

"The practice of devout deeds to commence," is illustrated by Prahlāda's famous statement from *Śrīmad Bhāgavata*:

To hear of Viṣṇu, praise, and contemplate,
To serve his feet, to worship, and prostrate,
To serve him and seek friendship sublime,
The soul in self surrender to resign.
If a man his devotion thus directs,
Firmly adhering to these nine aspects,
Devoutly to the Lord Viṣṇu addressed,
That one I ween in learning is the best.[5]

Verse Four: Six Signs of Love

ददाति प्रतिगृह्णाति गुह्यमाख्याति पृच्छति ।
भुङ्क्ते भोजयते चैव षड्विधं प्रीतिलक्षणम् ॥ ४ ॥

dadāti pratigṛhṇāti guhyamākhyāti pṛcchati |
bhuṅkte bhojayate caiva ṣaḍvidhaṃ prītilakṣaṇam || 4 ||

To receive and worthy gifts to offer,
To ask about deep subjects, and confer;
To offer food, on offered food to dine,
These six practices are of love the sign.

---

[5]Bhāg. 7.5.23-24.

The meaning is clear: the social intercourse, fond behavior, and pleasant conduct signify the outward expressions of mutual affection. I wonder why the commentary says very little on this verse. I suppose the meaning is clear, but I would have thought it was worth elaboration, friendship being such an interesting subject. One of the annotators lays a caution on not indulging in the above exchanges of affection with non-devotees, which seems a bit harsh, but I suppose it's a valid observation.

Verse Five: Deferential Conduct

Having provided a general illustration of affectionate behavior in the forgoing verse, the author proceeds on a consideration in reference to the deferential conduct prescribed towards devotees of varying levels of maturity.

कृष्णेति यस्य गिरि तं मनसाद्रियेत
दीक्षास्ति चेत्प्रणतिभिश्च भजन्तमीशम् ।
शुश्रूषया भजनविज्ञमनन्यमन्य-
निन्दादिशून्यहृदमीप्सितसङ्गलब्ध्या ॥ ५ ॥

kṛṣṇeti yasya giri taṃ manasādriyeta
dīkṣāsti cetpraṇatibhiśca bhajantamīśam |
śuśrūṣayā bhajanavijñamananyamanya-
nindādiśūnyahṛdamīpsitasaṅgalabdhyā || *5* ||

From whose speech the name of Kṛṣṇa is heard,
Shall in the mind be held in high regard;
The initiate, worshiping the Lord,
Should be with prostration fitly adored;
But one who has mature experience
In worship, should be held in reverence;
Who is from fault finding and vices free,
Is the best and most desired company.

Verse Six: Judgmental Restraint

Next the author, Śrī Rūpa, admonishes the reader, in case the above is taken solely on external consideration, to refrain from forming judgments on the basis of external appearances and manners of the devotee. He supplies an analogy, to which all pious people will attest.

दृष्टैः स्वभावजनितैर्वपुषश्च दोषै-
र्न प्राकृतत्वमिह भक्तजनस्य पश्येत।
गङ्गाम्भसां न खलु बुद्बुद्फेनपङ्कै-
र्ब्रह्मद्रवत्वमपगच्छति नीरधर्मैः ॥ ६ ॥

dṛṣṭaiḥ svabhāvajanitairvapuṣaśca doṣai-
rna prākṛtatvamiha bhaktajanasya paśyet|
gaṅgāmbhasāṃ na khalu budbudphenapaṅkai-
rbrahmadravatvamapagacchati nīradharmaiḥ|| 6 ||

Though natural and native faults there be
In the form and mein of a devotee,
It is not meet a votary to scan,
Since he is not an ordinary man.
Even as in the holy Gaṇgā's stream
Foam and bubbles and mud are often seen,
Yet by transubstantiation sublime,
She ever keeps her purity divine.

Śrī Kṛṣṇa says to Arjuna regarding the special prerogative afforded to the devotee, that any irregularities are not to be scrutinized too closely, since they are overcome by the devotee's resolve.

But even one immersed in awful sins,
If he my wholehearted worship begins,
Sure he a pious man is deemed to be,
Who has resolved thus deliberately.

He soon becomes a righteous man, and goes
To everlasting peace, and blest repose;
O son of Kuntī, proclaim and repeat,

My devotee never suffers defeat![6]

Verse Seven: Cause and Cure of Distaste

The cause is identified and the remedial measures proposed for an initial lack of taste for, or even aversion, to Śrī Kṛṣṇa's name, etc. The bilious distemper of the tongue which causes sugar to have a nasty taste is likened to the disorder of beginningless ignorance, resulting in an aversion to the naturally sweet relish of Kṛṣṇa and his name. Even as sugar is supposed to cure the distempered tongue and restore its appreciation of natural sweetness, so the daily repetition of Kṛṣṇa's name by its own inherent sweetness eradicates the bitter taste of ignorance.

> स्यात्कृष्णनामचरितादिसिताप्यविद्या-
> पित्तोपतप्तरसनस्य न रोचिका नु।
> किन्त्वादरादनुदिनं खलु सैव जुष्टा
> स्वाद्वी क्रमाद्भवति तद्गदमूलहन्त्री॥ ७ ॥

> *syāt kṛṣṇanāmacaritādisitāpyavidyā-*
> *pittopataptarasanasya na rocikā nu|*
> *kintvādarādanudinaṃ khalu saiva juṣṭā*
> *svādvī kramādbhavati tadgadamūlahantrī|| 7 ||*

> **The sweet relish of Kṛṣṇa's name and deeds,**
> **The malady of ignorance impedes;**
> **As the distempered tongue that bile secretes**
> **cannot apprehend the taste of sweets,**
> **So, sugar when administered, 'tis sure,**
> **Revives the sweet taste and effects the cure.**
> **Even so, when his name is daily sung,**
> **In adoration, flowing o'er the tongue,**
> **By degrees, in devotion resolute,**
> **Ignorance is destroyed down to the root.**

The Rāja Parīkṣit also makes the observation that the narratives of Śrī Hari, aside from other inestimable benefits, also provide the cure to the malady of worldly existence:

---

[6] *Bhagavad-gītā*, 9. 30-31.

Who but a ritual butcher would abstain,
From song which lauds Uttamaśloka's[7] fame!
Such song by ascetics is sung and rehearsed,
Who have o'ercome for worldliness the thirst;
Like some potent simple it cures all ills,
Captures the ear, the mind with rapture fills.[8]

Verse Eight: The Essence of Instruction

Śrī rūpa has dispatched the preliminaries:

1. the six urges,
2. the six detriments,
3. the six enhancements,
4. the six signs of mutual affection,
5. prescribed conduct towards devotees of varying degrees of maturity,
6. a caution is issued on the avoidance of forming judgments on the appearance and mein of a devotee, since to entertain animosity or disdain is unworthy and understood to be a fatal bar to progress in devotional disciplines,
7. the cause and remedy for laxity and want of taste is considered in the initial stages of practice.

Thus, by degrees, the essence of instruction is decocted, and, as indicated by the title of the work, Śrī Rūpa proposes that essence in the eighth verse in words something like these:

तन्नामरूपचरितादिसुकीर्तनानु-
स्मृत्योः क्रमेण रसनामनसी नियोज्य।
तिष्ठन् व्रजे तदनुरागिजनानुगामी
कालं नयेदखिलमित्युपदेशसारम॥ ८ ॥

---

[7]He who is praised by the finest verses, i.e. Kṛṣṇa.
[8]Bhāg.,10.1.4.

tannāmarūpacaritādisukīrtanānu-
smṛtyoḥ krameṇa rasanāmanasī niyojya|
tiṣṭhan vraje tadanurāgijanānugāmī
kālaṃ nayedakhilamityupadeśasāram|| 8 ||

His name, his beauty, and his deeds sublime,
To hear and sing of his glory divine,
And with the conscious faculty refined,
With the tongue, by degrees, to yoke the mind—
To dwell in Vraja and follow the ways
That his loving associate displays—
Thus spending all one's time in worship skilled,
The essence of all teachings is distilled.

Thus, the Nectar of Instruction is distilled.

Elsewhere, the author has formulated the inner and outward practice of meditation maintained by external discipline.

Recall Kṛṣṇa and that associate
Whose fond affection one would emulate;
The tidings of his deeds both hear and tell,
And always in, or upon Vraja dwell.

The aspirant, in his external form,
The external practices should perform,
But in his perfect form of certain kind,
(Conceived in the faculty of the mind),
He should render all timely services due,
And thus the Vraja-people's ways pursue.[9]

Again there is a verse from Śrī Rūpa's *Ocean of the Nectar of the Rapture of Devotion* that goes like this:

One who to constant worship is inclined,
With articles perceived within the mind,
Tho' far beyond the mind, and speech, and sense,
Hari grants him his direct audience.[10]

---

[9]*Brs.*, 1.2.294-5.

[10]*Brs.*, 1.2.182:

mānasenopacāreṇa paricarya hariṃ sadā |
pare vāṅmanasā'gamyaṃ taṃ sākṣātpratipedire ||

As for the perfect form of certain kind conceived within the mind, the meditation manuals provide a self-meditation something like this,

> The identity in the mind perceived,
> Of profound aspiration is conceived;
> As one of her dear friends amid the train
> Of Rādhā's dear companions, and again,
> To render intimate attendance due,
> Their orders and their gestures to pursue;
> With gems, garments, and embellishments dight,
> Mercifully bestowed and coloured bright.[11]

Verse Nine: Hierarchy of Divine Abodes

Now, the author begins a hierarchical survey of the divine abodes, arriving by degrees at Rādhākuṇḍa.

> वैकुण्ठाज्जनितो वरा मधुपुरी तत्रापि रासोत्सवा-
> द्वृन्दारण्यमुदारपाणिरमणात्तत्रापि गोवर्धनः ।
> राधाकुण्डमिहापि गोकुलपतेः प्रेमामृताप्लवना-
> त्कुर्यादस्य विराजतो गिरितटे सेवां विवेकी न कः ॥ ९ ॥

> *vaikuṇṭhājjanito varā madhupurī tatrāpi rāsotsavā-*
> *dvṛndāraṇyamudārapāṇiramaṇāttatrāpi govardhanaḥ|*
> *rādhākuṇḍamihāpi gokulapateḥ premāmṛtāplavanā-*
> *tkuryādasya virājato giritaṭe sevāṃ vivekī na kaḥ|| 9 ||*

> **Surpassing even Vaikuṇṭha on earth,**
> **Is Mathurā, city where he took birth;**
> **But Vṛndāvan that glory does surpass,**
> **Where celebrated he the festive Rās;**
> **Mount Govardhan that excellence exceeds,**
> **Where the lofty handed enacts his deeds.**
> **But Rādhā's lake surpasses all above,**
> **Flooded with the Lord of Gokula's love.**

---

[11] *Arcanā-paddhati*, ?

What wise man would not serve and there abide,
At that lake which adorns the mountainside?

Vaikuṇṭha is the divine eternal realm of Hari beyond time and space, birth, growth, etc., where he dwells with his Goddess consorts and attendants. Mathurā excels insofar as it is the place where he deigns to be born in the guise of man. Vṛndāvana surpasses Mathurā as the place of the Rāsa dance. Govardhana is the scene of a still more wonderful variety of amorous diversions. Śrī Raghunātha Dāsa, in his *Govardhanāśraya-daśaka*, says:

How blessed is Mount Govardhan divine,
Where, with Saṅkarṣaṇa, he tends the kine;
Where, with friends like Śrīdāma, he regales,
And sings delightsome melodious scales;
Where he to a bosky grotto resorts,
To dally with Rādhā in amorous sports.
Who is that pious one who would not take
Refuge at Govardhan, and dwelling make?[12]

There is also a parallel verse in *Vraja-vilāsa-stava*: more dear than Vaikuṇṭha is Dvārakā; more so Mathurā, and in Mathurā Vraja stands superlative.

The city Dvāravatī is more dear
Than Vaikuṇṭha, since he fondly dwells there;
With brother and with sons the Lord abides,
And a multitude of beautiful brides,
Who each with a radiant lustre gleam,
That dims a hundred Śrī Goddesses sheen.
More dear, though, is the field of love on earth,
Mathurā city where Hari took birth;
And in the environs, preeminent,
The meadows and the cowherd settlement
Of Vraja, where Lord Hari freely plays.
I thus adore divine Vraja always.[13]

In his *Rādhākuṇḍāṣṭaka*, Raghunātha Dāsa prays for refuge at Rādhākuṇḍa:

---

[12] *Govardhanāśraya-daśaka*, 9.
[13] *Vraja-vilāsa-stava*, 5.

That lovely lake abounds with lotus flowers,
Surcharging all around with sweet odours.
It's filled with scented waters that charm the eye,
Where the delightsome couple daily vie
In water sports, splashing with eager strokes,
Which passion's frenzy in them both evokes.
Thus with their dear companions, every day,
In the water and on the banks they play.
May I, by gracious favour, refuge take
At Rādhā's beautiful and fragrant lake.[14]

Verse Ten: Hierarchy of Bhaktas

Having by gradation proposed the prefered place of worship and ultimate attainment, the author proceeds to enumerate another gradation in respect to persons, and, as the foregoing text established Rādhākuṇḍa as the ultimate place, so by identifying Rādhā herself with her lake, the following text establishes Rādhā as the preeminent repository of Kṛṣṇa's love. Again, by rhetorical flair, the author questions, Who would not seek to take refuge there?

कर्मिभ्यः परितो हरेः प्रियतया व्यक्तिं ययुर्ज्ञानिन-
स्तेभ्यो ज्ञानविमुक्तभक्तिपरमाः प्रेमैकनिष्ठास्ततः ।
तेभ्यस्ताः पशुपालपङ्कजदृशस्ताभ्यो ऽपि सा राधिका
प्रेष्ठा तद्वदियं तदीयसरसी तां नाश्रयेत्कः कृती ॥ १० ॥

karmibhyaḥ parito hareḥ priyatayā vyaktiṃ yayurjñānina-
stebhyo jñānavimuktabhaktiparamāḥ premaikaniṣṭhāstataḥ|
tebhyastāḥ paśupālapaṅkajadṛśastābhyo 'pi sā rādhikā
preṣṭhā tadvadiyaṃ tadīyasarasī tāṃ nāśrayetkaḥ kṛtī|| 10 ||

The wise man is regarded more than he
Engaged in rituals, by Lord Hari;
Yet dearer they who freed by wisdom are
And view divine devotion best by far.

[14] *Rādhākuṇḍāṣṭaka*, 8.

Dearer still are others who rise above,
Firmly fixed in exclusively pure love.
But dearest are the cowherd damosels,
Lotus-eyed; midst whom Rādhikā excels.
And as dear as she is, dear is her lake,
What pious one would not there refuge take?

Elsewhere, divine Rūpa enumerates twenty five prominent attributes, in appreciation of which Kṛṣṇa himself is captivated.

Vṛndāvan's empress, with virtues aplenty
Is endowed: here are just five and twenty.

Most sweet, of tender age, and restless eyed,
Bright smiles; with lines of fortune beautified;
Her scent Mādhava does intoxicate;
In arts of music she is consummate.

Of charming speech, of subtle lively wit,
Extremely modest, and compassionate,
She has cunning wiles, and keen dexterity
In diverse tasks; exceeding shy is she.

In showing respect she's most diligent,
Possessed of fortitude and firm intent.
A character profound she does display;
Dexterous in all the arts of amorous play.

She is the zenith of ecstatic bliss,
And the abode where Gokul's pure love is.
Her lustrous fame thro'out the world is known,
The object of her elders' affection;

She practices submission to her friends.
Of Kṛṣṇa's lovers she alone transcends.
And thus by her accomplishments and skill,
She keeps Keśava subject to her will.[15]

The meditation on Rādhā can be found in many texts, but here is one from the *Sanatkumāra-saṃhitā*, often quoted in the manuals. Following the meditation on Kṛṣṇa, the meditation on Rādhā proceeds in words like these,

---

[15]Rūpa Gosvāmin, *Ujjvala-nīlamaṇi*, 4.11-15.

Now, contemplate, on Kṛṣṇa's left hand side,
Rādhikā, in the glow of beauty's pride;
She wears a fine flowing garment of blue;
Her fair limbs bear of ductile gold the hue;

And with a flimsy silk translucent veil,
She does her smiling lotus-face conceal.
Upto her lover's face her glances rise,
Like the moon-bird, with thirsty gazing eyes;

Between her thumb and finger she does hold
A tasty betal wrap with areca nut rolled.
Raising the Tāmbul to her lover's face,
In his lotus-mouth the treat she does place.

Lovely strands of bright pearl necklaces rest
Upon her ample and protruding breast;
Her midriff is compact, sturdy her thighs;
Decked with a tinkling belt with golden ties.

She is further, with golden earings dight,
Anklets on feet, and toes with toe-rings bright.
Thus her enchanting beauty shows the gleam
And depth of lustre and of pearly sheen.[16]

Verse Eleven: Rādhā's Lake

Why is Rādhākuṇḍa exalted above all other holy and sanctified places? As a holy site, what benefit or fruit might be expected to accrue from serving and taking a holy dip? In text nine Rādhākuṇḍa was exalted by reason of the particular variety of pastimes that occur there. In text ten Rādhā was exalted among all loving devotees of Kṛṣṇa, and her lake was identified with her in terms of being favoured by Hari and endowed with her own qualities of mercy, grace etc. In the final text, eleven, the author states the rarity of the opportunity given to bathe there, even for those who might be considered devotees, and asserts that the fruit of serving and taking a dip in Rādhākuṇḍa engenders a love similar to the love of which Rādhā herself is the repository.

---

[16] *Sanatkumāra-saṃhitā*, 36.63-68.

कृष्णस्योच्चैः प्रणयवसतिः प्रेयसीभ्योऽपि राधा
कुण्डं चास्या मुनिभिरभितस्तादृगेव व्यधायि।
यत्प्रेष्ठैरप्यलमसुलभं किं पुनर्भक्तिभाजां
तत्प्रेमेदं सकृदपि सरः स्नातुराविष्करोति॥ ११ ॥

kṛṣṇasyoccaiḥ praṇayavasatiḥ preyasībhyo'pi rādhā
kuṇḍaṃ cāsyā munibhirabhitastādṛgeva vyadhāyi|
yatpreṣṭhairapyalamasulabhaṃ kiṃ punarbhaktibhājāṃ
tatpremedaṃ sakṛdapi saraḥ snāturāviṣkaroti|| 11 ||

Of all of Kṛṣṇa's loves, Rādhā is best,
And even as is she, her lake is blest;
And ancient sages in their hymns declare,
Attainment of that lake is very rare,
Even for his devout and loving train,
Since whoso bathes in that lake shall attain
By favour which the lake itself confers,
A fond love like the love that Rādhā bears.

Raghunātha Dāsa also states in his *Rādhākuṇḍāṣṭaka*, regarding the fruit of serving the holy lake,

Some people here have by their service won
Great mercy from the cowherd chief's dear son,
But worshiping this fragrant lake divine,
Within sprouts up a celestial vine,
Which then does suddenly burst into flower—
The service of my empress in the bower.
May I, by gracious favour, refuge take
By Rādhā's beautiful and fragrant lake.[17]

Even Kṛṣṇa himself bathes there to gain the good grace of Rādhā, as Raghunātha Dāsa further observes,

Even Agha's great foe himself does crave
His limbs within that fragrant lake to lave;
And makes his vows, and prays he might possess,

[17] Raghunātha Dāsa Gosvāmin, *Rādhākuṇḍāṣṭaka*, 5.

A merciful glance from his dear goddess.
May I, by gracious favour, refuge take
By Rādhā's beautiful and fragrant lake.[18]

[18]Raghunātha Dāsa Gosvāmin, *Rādhākuṇḍāṣṭaka*, 3.

Raghunātha Dāsa Gosvāmī: Instructions to My Mind

Verse One: Extraordinary Love

Well, having sped through brief surveys of *Śikṣāṣṭaka* and *Upadeśāmṛta*, it now follows that we complete the triad of instruction manuals with Śrī Raghunātha Dāsa Gosvāmī's *Manah-śikṣā*, consisting of eleven plus one stanzas (12), or verses, *śloka*-s, texts, couplets, or whatever is preferable, which as the title suggests, take the form of lessons, sermons, exhortations and admonitions—ostensibly to himself, but intended for anyone who is interested in learning what he is endeavoring to convey. As with the foregoing texts, the instruction derived from *Manah-śikṣā* is not about theology, metaphysics or the analysis of categories, but pertains to esoteric practices of mystic contemplation, the appropriate disposition, and right conduct, etc. In text one he addresses his own mind, clasping his feet, as "inner brother," in conciliatory terms, not as the strict disciplinarian, but with deference to coax, cajole, and conjure and bring it round to a willing and ready compliance. An objecter may ask, how does the mind have feet?–to which it might be said, well if one is going to address the mind personally, why not ascribe feet, to draw out the metaphor? He (the author) proceeds to enumerate eight articles which he would have the mind (or the auditor) cultivate; an *apūrva*[1] love, which is to say, an extraordinary love for the ensuing eight arti-

[1] Lit. "unprecedented."

cles which are as follows: 1. the guru, 2. the cowherd settlement, 3. the cowherds, 4. pious people, 5. the earth gods, ie, *brāhmaṇas*, 6. the initiation *mantra*, 7. the holy name, and 8. the shelter of Rādhā and Kṛṣṇa.

गुरौ गोष्ठे गोष्ठालयिषु सुजने भूसुरगणे
स्वमन्त्रे श्रीनाम्नि व्रजनवयुवद्वन्द्वशरणे ।
सदा दम्भं हित्वा कुरु रतिमपूर्वामतितरा-
मये स्वान्तर्भ्रातश्चटुभिरभियाचे धृतपदः ॥ १ ॥

gurau goṣṭhe goṣṭhālayiṣu sujane bhūsuragaṇe
svamantre śrīnāmni vrajanavayuvadvandvaśaraṇe |
sadā dambhaṃ hitvā kuru ratimapūrvāmatitarā-
maye svāntarbhrātaścaṭubhirabhiyāce dhṛtapadaḥ || *1* ||

O mind, I hold your feet and supplicate,
To give up arrogance of high estate;
Extraordinary love to cultivate,
For teacher, and the holy pasture land;
Cowherds, the pious, the god-like *brahman* band;
My secret *mantra*, and the name divine,
And refuge with the young couple benign. (1)

As for cultivating friendship with one's own mind, Kṛṣṇa says to Arjuna in the *Gītā*,

Let each self then, the self by self upraise,
But let him not the self by self debase;
For self alone is of the self the friend,
The self also a foe who may contend.

The self is the friend of the self for him
Who by the self the self has conquered been;
But for the self that is unconquered, know,
The self alone is of the self the foe.[2]

Elsewhere, in another text, Śrī Dāsa Gosvāmī has expressed a similar conceit in his *Self Imposed Vows* (*Sva-niyama-daśaka*),

[2] *Bhagavad-gītā* (Bg.), 6.5-6.

May my devoted affection adhere
To preceptor, *mantra*, and the name dear;
To Svarūp, and Rūpa, and all his train,
To his elder may I fond love maintain;
May I, with love, be ever worshiping,
Gandharva's fair lake, and the mountain king,
The pasture lands and Madhu's citadel,
And voteries who in Gokula dwell.[3]

Verse Two: Beyond Good and Evil

A caution and prescription, and a confirmation.

न धर्मं नाधर्मं श्रुतिगणनिरुक्तं किल कुरु
व्रजे राधाकृष्णप्रचुरपरिचर्यामिह तनु ।
शचीसूनुं नन्दीश्वरपतिसुतत्वे गुरुवरं
मुकुन्दप्रेष्ठत्वे स्मर पदमजस्रं मनु मनः ॥ २ ॥

na dharmaṃ nādharmaṃ śrutigaṇaniruktaṃ kila kuru
vraje rādhākṛṣṇapracuraparicaryāmiha tanu |
śacīsūnuṃ nandīśvarapatisutatve guruvaraṃ
mukundapreṣṭhatve smara padamajasraṃ manu manaḥ || 2 ||

Do not to vice and virtue pay much heed,
As has in ancient scripture been decreed;
Nay, rather serve within Vṛndāvan's grove
Rādhā and Kṛṣṇa, ardently with love;
And always hold that Śacī's darling son
Is Nanda's son indeed, for they are one;
Know my teacher to Mukunda is dear,
O mind, do you ever his feet revere. (2)

The author admonishes his mind to avoid preoccupation with ethical questions of virtue and vice pertaining to scriptural prescriptions and prohibitions. Kṛṣṇa concludes his discourse to Uddhava on the determination of virtue and vice in words like these,

[3]Raghunātha Dāsa, *Svaniyama-daśaka*, 1.

Why say too much on virtue and on vice?
Let what has been said up to this suffice;
To transcend the distinction twixt the two,
Is verily the sign of real virtue.[4]

Śrī Caitanyadeva is reported to have made the observation in regard to the differential disposition.

By differential outlook is defined,
Blest and unblest, a function of the mind;
This good, that bad. Such distinctions to make
Is but to be in error and mistake.[5]

It is better to serve Rādhā and Kṛṣṇa in the grove with ardent love:

In Vṛndāvan beneath the wishing tree,
A temple stands under the canopy;
Inlaid with precious gems, the stately dome
Enshrines a massy golden lion throne;
Upon that throne the loving pair divine,
Śrī Rādhikā and Govinda recline;
While all around companions on them wait;
This scene I call to mind and meditate.[6]

Prabodhānanda Sarasvatī provides a meditation on Śrī Caitanyadeva,

Whose wide shoulders are broad and leonine;
Whose cheeks swell with the sweetest smiles sublime;
Whose person undergoes varieties,
Of ineffable loving ecstasies;
Who softly shines as when petals unfold
The interior of a lotus gold.
May he grant you protection and delight,
In whom Rādhā and Mādhava unite.[7]

In Dhyānacandra's manual we also find this,

[4]Bhāg., 11.19.45
[5]Cc., 3.4.170.
[6]Cc., 1.1.16.
[7]Prabodhānanda Sarasvatī, *Caitanya-candrāmṛta*, 13.

Meditate upon him whose sable curls
Are bound up in a knot with strands of pearls;
Caitanya radiates a golden gleam,
Surrounded by his followers, aglow;
With fine raiment and embellishments dight,
And flower wreaths and gold necklaces bright;
He does in dance of rapture sweetly move;
In garb and beauty like the god of Love.[8]

My teacher is dear to Mukunda, the holy writ says,

This wisdom is manifest and bestowed,
On him who loves his Guru as his God.[9]

Verse Three: Enjoined or Impassioned Bhakti

In the previous verse, Raghunātha, addressing his mind, urged it to reject blind adherence to rules of virtue and vice. Anticipating the question, "By what rule then must one direct one's conduct?" the author adduces some basic principles for guidance. The practice of devotional disciplines proceeds along two distinct paths; one is impelled and inspired by scriptural ratiocination to have a keen regard for rules and regulations. The other is driven by an eager curiosity to imbibe the spontaneous feeling of love that obtains between Kṛṣṇa and his associates—Kṛṣṇa being the object, the associates the subject or repositories, of spontaneous love.[10] Ostensibly there is no distinction between this or that path, since this one is characterised by inner contemplation on Kṛṣṇa's names, beauty, attributes, and exploits. Śrī Rūpa sums up, saying,

The hearing, recital, and all the forms
Of *Vaidhi* practises with this conforms;
Thus the wise and learned on this declare,
In both mindsets these practises are there.[11]

[8] Dhyānacandra, *Gaura-govindārcana-smaraṇa-paddhati*, 49.
[9] *Śvetāśvatara Upaniṣad*, 6.23.
[10] Vide the notes to Rūpa's *Upadeśāmṛta*, Verse Eight.
[11] Brs., 1.2.296.

यदीच्छेरावासं व्रजभुवि सरागं प्रतिजनु-
र्युवद्वन्द्वं तच्चेत्परिचरितुमारादभिलषेः ।
स्वरूपं श्रीरूपं सगणमिह तस्याग्रजमपि
स्फुटं प्रेम्णा नित्यं स्मर नम तदा त्वं शृणु मनः ॥ ३ ॥

yadīccherāvāsaṃ vrajabhuvi sarāgaṃ pratijanu-
ryuvadvandvaṃ taccetparicaritumārādabhilaṣeḥ |
svarūpaṃ śrīrūpaṃ sagaṇamiha tasyāgrajamapi
sphutaṃ premnā nityaṃ smara nama tadā tvaṃ śṛṇu manaḥ || 3 ||

Should you with love in Vraja wish to dwell
From birth to birth, O mind, hear what I tell;
And if you long the loving pair to serve,
These are the ways and means you must observe.
Fondly recall and bow in reverence due
To Svarūp, Rūpa, and his elder too,
And all the blest society that stay
In Vraja, worshiping thro'out the day. (3)

Homage to the six Gosvāmins, who are the expositors and exemplars of spontaneous love, including the author,

Hail Rūpa, Raghunāth and Sanātan!
Hail Gopāl Bhaṭṭ, and Tapan Miśra's son!
Hail Jīva Gosāi, Rūpa's fond nephew,
I bow in reverence to all of you.

Verse Four: The Impediments

Now, Raghunātha proceeds to enumerate some of the impediments on the path of spontaneous love which cause the mind to be diverted from its course.

असद्वार्त्ता वेश्या विसृज मतिसर्वस्वहरणीः
कथा मुक्तिव्याघ्या न शृणु किल सर्वात्मगिलनीः ।
अपि त्यक्त्वा लक्ष्मीपतिरतिमितो व्योमनयनीम्

व्रजे राधाकृष्णौ स्वरतिमणिदौ त्वं भज मनः ॥ ४॥

asadvārttā veśyā visṛja matisarvasvaharaṇīḥ
kathā muktivyāghryā na śṛṇu kila sarvātmagilanīḥ |
api tyaktvā lakṣmīpatiratimito vyomanayanīm
vraje rādhākṛṣṇau svaratimaṇidau tvaṃ bhaja manaḥ || 4||

Reject the harlot, Vain-talk, who by stealth,
Deprives you of your intellectual wealth;
Of soul's emancipation hear no more,
Which, tigress like, your being will devour;
And even forsake love for Lakṣmī's Lord,
Who draws you to his heaven for reward.
Nay, rather, O my mind! I do implore,
That Rādhā-Kṛṣṇa only you adore;
For they confer on those who worship them,
Of their own love supreme the rarest gem. (4)

Idle and frivolous talk is likened to a courtesan who dissipates her client's wealth; implying the wealth of discrimination here. Discourses on the theme of liberation—which indicates absorption of one's being into the undifferentiated, ineffable Brahman—is compared to a ferocious hungry tigress, ready to devour the soul. Then, in the exuberance of exclusive love directed to the sweet rustic forms of Rādha and Kṛṣṇa in Vraja, he advises caution in regard to becoming attracted to Kṛṣṇa in his grand majestic form as Nārāyaṇa, the spouse of Goddess Lakṣmī, who, despite being prized above himself, draws and entices the aspirant to his transcendent realm above the sky, which prejudices or compromises the attainment of the fond and simple love of Kṛṣṇa, son of the cowherd Nanda. He concludes the last line by exhorting his mind (and the reader's) to cultivate exclusive worship of Rādhā and Kṛṣṇa who, in the cowherd settlement of Vraja, bestow the rare gem of spontaneous love.

The sage Satyavrata, in his Dāmodara Octet, extracted from the *Padma Purāṇa*, sings,

O Lord of boons, I do not seek from thee
Liberation in whatever degree,
Nor do I any boon from thee require.

This, O my Lord, is my only desire,
That this, thy form as the young cowherd boy
May in my mind remain; what other joy
Could equal this great blessing, or exceed?
I have, indeed, for other boons no need.

This lotus-face of thine, of beauty rare,
Is framed by curly locks of sable hair,
With crimson patches that clearly confess,
Where thou art kissed by the fond cowherdess,
With rosy lips as *bimba* berries soft,
She kisses thee both many times and oft.
Let this vision within my mind remain;
Enough, O Lord of any other gain.[12]

Verse Five: Help from Kṛṣṇa's Companions

Here Raghunātha encourages followers to take as saviors the associates of Kṛṣṇa and appeal to them for succor and aid.

असच्चेष्टाकष्टप्रदविकटपासालिभिरिह
प्रकामं कामादिप्रकटपथपातिव्यतिकरैः ।
गले बद्ध्वा हन्येऽहमिति बकभिद्वर्त्मपगणे
कुरु त्वं फुत्कारानवति स यथा त्वां मन इतः ॥ ५ ॥

asacceṣṭākaṣṭapradavikaṭapāsālibhiriha
prakāmaṃ kāmādiprakaṭapathapātivyatikaraiḥ |
gale baddhvā hanye'hamiti bakabhidvartmapagaṇe
kuru tvaṃ phutkārānavati sa yathā tvāṃ mana itaḥ || 5 ||

The wayside thieves, Desire and his train,
The noose of vain endeavours, causing pain,
Have flung about my neck, and so I die.
O mind! to save us you must loudly cry
For succor to the guardians of the way,

[12] *Dāmodarāṣṭaka*, 4-5.

The votaries of Baka's enemy;
And they will surely rescue you from grief,
And set you free, affording swift relief. (5)

In honour to the votaries of Viṣṇu a well known verse salutes and praises their virtues,

All hail, all hail! to Viṣṇu's votaries,
The incarnated wish fulfilling trees,
And oceans vast of extreme compassion,
Who to the base grant purification.[13]

Elsewhere, Raghunātha, in a similar strain, opens his *Vraja-vilāsa-stava* with these words,

I'm caught and bound with tight and sturdy ropes,
Of honour and distinction's ardent hopes;
And held in durance by the highwaymen,
Called Desire for Pleasure and for Gain;
May the patrol guards of the enemy
Of Agha, loose my bonds and set me free.[14]

Verse Six: Avoidance of Deceit and Hypocrisy

Having entreated, exhorted, and persuaded, and thereby, having mollified his mind, the author now takes on a more peremptory tone and expresses his abhorrence and disgust, and abominates the vices of hypocrisy and double dealing. Rebuking and upbraiding his laxity, he draws a striking contrast between the immaculate perception of Rādhā and Kṛṣṇa's eternal love sports, and the baseness of vain pride and duplicity.

अरे चेतः प्रोद्यत्कपटकुटिनाटीभरखर-
क्षरन्मूत्रे स्नात्वा दहसि कथमात्मानमपि माम् ।
सदा त्वं गान्धर्वागिरिधरपदप्रेमविलसत-

[13]Unsure of original source.
[14]Raghunātha Dāsa, *Vraja-vilāsa-stava*, 1.

सुधाम्भोधे स्नात्वा स्वमपि नितरां मां च सुखय ॥ ६ ॥

are cetaḥ prodyatkapaṭakuṭināṭībharakhara-
kṣaranmūtre snātvā dahasi kathamātmānamapi mām |
sadā tvaṃ gāndharvāgiridharapadapremavilasat-
sudhāmbhodhe snātvā svamapi nitarāṃ māṃ ca sukhaya || 6||

O foolish mind! wherefore do you allow
Dissembling and hypocrisy to grow?
Which scorches, and deprives us both of bliss,
Like bathing in a stream of donkey's piss!
Nay, rather, take a dip in that bright sea,
Ambrosial love for Gāndharvā and he
Who lifted up a mountain on his hand.
This is, O mind, what you should understand.
Do this, and then the sure result shall be
The highest joy to you, and bliss to me. (6)

Verse Seven: Overcoming the Desire for Fame

The desire for fame, honour, and distinction is represented as one of the final vices to be overcome due to its stubborn persistence. The means to overcome this vain pride is prescribed as sincere and deferential service and attendance on the heroic generals who are the recipients, repositories, and agents of divine grace, whose propitiation secures the attenuation of this vice.

प्रतिष्ठाशा धृष्टश्वपचरमणी मे हृदि नटेत्
कथं साधु प्रेमा स्पृशति शुचिरेतन्ननु मनः ।
सदा त्वं सेवस्व प्रभुदयितसामन्तमतुलं
यथा तां निष्काश्य त्वरितमिह तं वेशयति सः ॥ ७ ॥

pratiṣṭhāśā dhṛṣṭaśvapacaramaṇī me hṛdi naṭet
kathaṃ sādhu premā spṛśati śuciretannanu manaḥ |
sadā tvaṃ sevasva prabhudayitasāmantamatulaṃ
yathā tāṃ niṣkāśya tvaritamiha taṃ veśayati saḥ || 7 ||

So long as you preeminence desire,
For honours and distinction still aspire,
Which like a base born shameless wench, within
Your bosom dances, tainting it with sin.
How can that pure love sanctify your heart,
While she there plays, refusing to depart?
O mind, with profound regard you must serve
A favorite of the Lord without reserve,
And he will banish her without delay.
Then seat love within your heart straight away.

The gradual development and accomplishment of ecstatic love is treated in the *Caitanya-caritāmṛta*, where Śrī Caitanyadeva is represented as delivering a parable on the the creeping vine of Love. The ensuing passage is an idiomatic rendering in blank verse, which is to say iambic pentameter lines sans the endline rhyming.

Some fortunate soul, having wandered through
This world in many lifetimes, may receive
From preceptor and Kṛṣṇa's potent grace,
The fertile seed of love-joy's creeping vine.
Then, like a gardener, that seed he sows;
He sprinkles there the vivifying drops,
Upon the seed, which here does represent
The hearing and recital of his deeds.
And as the creeper grows with fair increase,
It spreads beyond the river Virāja,
And pierces through the atmosphere supreme,
Then onward, ever upward, finds at last,
The region of Goloka Vṛndāvan.
The vine embraces there the wishing tree
Of Kṛṣṇa's feet and secures refuge there.
Thus in repose it spreads its tendrils round,
And many fruits and flowers does produce.
The gardener still with attentive care,
The same nourishing waters pours amain,
Of daily hearing, and such discipline.
Vaiṣṇav offence is the mad pachyderm,
Who tramples down and withers all the vine,
Therefore the keeper, diligent, will make

A stockade or enclosure all around,
To keep the elephant offences out.
But, if from the creeper's vigorous growth,
Wild and unwanted offshoots should result,
These represent the extraneous hopes
For worldly pleasure and liberation,
And many more, which cannot here be told—
Such as the vice of forbidden conduct,
A duplicitous conceit, and cruelty
To other beings, and lascivious greed;
And hankering for rank and eminence.
These are some of the wild unwanted growths,
Which if suffered to flourish and increase,
Sprinkled and tended by that same regime,
Deprive the main trunk of its nourishment,
And then the vine of love will stunted be.
From the beginning, the good gardener,
Will prune th'unwanted growths with diligence;
Then unrestricted, the main trunk will grow,
And to Vṛndāvan ultimately go.[15]

Verse Eight: Kṛṣṇa's Grace

Raghunātha affirms that, after all, in the endeavours to overcome obstacles, and improve one's disposition, hitherto discussed, ultimately all success relies on the good grace of Kṛṣṇa.

यथा दुष्टत्वं मे दवयति शठस्यापि कृपया
यथा मह्यं प्रेमामृतमपि ददात्युज्ज्वलमसौ ।
यथा श्रीगान्धर्वाभजनविधये प्रेरयति मां
तथा गोष्ठे काक्वा गिरिधरमिह त्वं भज मनः ॥ ८ ॥

yathā duṣṭatvaṃ me davayati śaṭhasyāpi kṛpayā
yathā mahyaṃ premāmṛtamapi dadātyujjvalamasau |
yathā śrīgāndharvābhajanavidhaye prerayati māṃ

[15] Kṛṣṇadāsa Kavirāja, *Caitanya-caritāmṛtra*, 2.19.

tathā goṣṭhe kākvā giridharamiha tvaṃ bhaja manaḥ || 8 ||

Just as the worst of recreants am I,
He, by his grace, my heart can rectify;
E'en as he does his sweet mercy bestow,
The ambrosia of his love to know;
Just as in worship of Gāndharvā fair
He prompts me to engage with devout care,
Thus, O my mind, while in this cowherd land,
To him who held a mountain on his hand,
Entreat in plaintive tones and broken voice,
That you may worship thus, and so rejoice.

The expression of humility here has been analysed in the notes to *Śikṣāṣṭaka* 3. Śrī Rūpa provides a pair of couplets in his *Utkalikā-vallarī*, which illustrate the plaintive petition, besieging and beseeching thus,

O tender child of cowherd chief, O hear,
I bow down in pleading and ardent prayer;
Make me the object of the compassion,
Of her who is of Vraja's dames the crown.

O Goddess Urjā, in piteous tone,
And earnest praise, I make my purpose known;
May I be graced by him who Baka slew,
Considering that I belong to you.[16]

Verse Nine: Recollections

Having thus admonished his mind, now with blandishment, now with threat, the author proceeds on a new theme.

मदीशानाथत्वे व्रजविपिनचन्द्रं व्रजवने-
श्वरिं तां नाथत्वे तदतुलसखीत्वे तु ललिताम् ।
विशाखां शिक्षालीवितरणगुरुत्वे प्रियसरो-

[16]Uv., 19-20.

गिरिन्द्रौ तत्प्रेक्षाललितरतिदत्वे स्मर मनः ॥ ९ ॥

madīśānāthatve vrajavipinacandraṃ vrajavane-
śvariṃ tāṃ nāthatve tadatulasakhītve tu lalitām |
viśākhāṃ śikṣālīvitaraṇagurutve priyasaro-
girindrau tatprekṣālalitaratidatve smara manaḥ || 9 ||

O mind, consider what I now shall say,
And heed the mystery that I convey.
My queen the mistress is of Vraja's Lord,
And he by Vraja's empress is adored;
Lalitā, their confidante without peer,
And Viśākhā, their preceptor is most dear.
Remember, too, that merely the sight
Of that dear lake wherein they take delight,
And Govardhan, of holy mounts the king,
The ecstasy of love's rapture can bring.

The attributes and the meditation on the beauty of Rādhā was supplied with *Upadeśāmṛta* text 10 in the notes. Now follows the four and sixty divine attributes of Kṛṣṇa enumerated by Śrī Rūpa in the *Bhakti-rasāmṛta-sindhu.*[17]

Our hero is of exquisite beauty,
Marked with the signs of every dignity;
Illustrious, and radiant, and strong,
Youthful, and versed in many a diverse tongue;

Of truthful speech and pleasing utterance,
Possessed of the most charming eloquence,
In scholarship and learning erudite,
A profound intellect and lively wit,

Skilful in arts, adroit and dexterous,
Grateful, in keeping vows most sedulous,
Mindful of time, and place, and personage,
Observant of the truth of scripture's page;

[17]Brs., 2.1.23-42.

Immaculately pure and self subdued,
With constancy and tolerance endued,
Forgiving, and profound, of steadfast mind,
Equanimous, magnanimous and kind;

Righteous, heroic and most merciful,
With due deference very respectful,
Compliant, meek, endued with modesty,
Protective of those who seek sanctuary;

Possessed of happiness and the true friend
Of the devotee, love bound,who extends
Blessed auspiciousness to everyone,
Puissant, and of the most worthy renown;

Who rouses all the world to love's passion,
Ready to show good people compassion;
Who charms all women, and is right worthy
Of worship; of growing prosperity;

Preeminent, endowed with lordliness;
Such attributes as Hari does possess,
Of high renown, that up to fifty go,
Like a profound and boundless ocean show,

Whence tiny drops and particles endue
The ordinary soul with some virtue.
But only in the supreme Lord are found,
Their fullest manifestation profound.

In the *Padma*, addressing Parvatī,
The peacock-blue throated divinity,
Recounted Hari's qualities divine,
Such as, the Lord who does with beauty shine,
More than a million Cupids in their prime.

Now five more qualities to some degree
Are seen in the mountain divinity,
And others; as he who always remaians
In his own form and his nature maintains,

Omniscient and having eternal youth,
A form comprised of knowledge, bliss, and truth,
Endowed with the full power and extent,

Of mystic perfection's accomplishment.

Now five more divine qualities are there,
Which Lakṣmī's Lord alone with him does share,
He is of ineffable power possessed,
Millions of universes are compressed
Within his body, and of each descent,
He is the seed; his enemies are sent
To salvation when they by him are slain.
And those who in their own self bliss remain,
Are drawn by his wonderful qualities—
Such are Kṛṣṇa's fair graces and beauties.

Kṛṣṇa himself is like an ocean full
Of wave-like exploits, sweetly wonderful;
He is encompassed by dear friends who bear
A loving sweetness beyond all compare,

The sweet melody of his flute inspires
The minds in all three worlds with soft desires,
And by his sweetest beauty, unsurpassed,
All living things are into wonder cast.

The meditation on Kṛṣṇa's form and beauty is found in the *Sanatkumāra Saṃhitā*,

Now, best of twice-born ones, I will proclaim,
How *mantra* meditation to maintain;
Kṛṣṇa is clad in robes of yellow hue,
His body is of cloud compexion blue.

He displays two arms, and is with garlands dight,
And wears a crown of peacock feathers bright;
His restless roving glances roll around,
His hair is with Karṇikār flowers bound;

With sandal paste mixed with vermilion red,
A fine *tilak* marking adorns his head,
He has bright ornamental pendants hung,
From his ears that shine like the baby sun.

His handsome cheeks are with sweat drops bedewed,
He transfers betel leaf which he has chewed,

Into the mouth of his beloved it goes,
With histrionic motions of eyebrows.

And the tip of his fine prominent nose,
With a big pendant and shiny pearl glows.
His teeth shine like the moonlight radiant white,
His luscious lips like *bimba* berries bright.

His arms with armlets, wrists with bracelets shine,
With signet rings on his soft fingers fine;
His bamboo flute in his left hand he holds,
The other a lotus. A sash of gold

Adorns his ample loins, and tinkling sweet,
A pair of sounding anklets on his feet.
Immersed in the rapturous ecstasies
Of love, and with rolling and restless eyes,

With his beloved he makes amorous jokes,
Joying himself, laughter in her he provokes.

Thus under the fair and bright canopy
On the lion throne, 'neath the wishing tree,
In Vrindavan on Kṛṣṇa meditate,
Sitting with his empress in regal state.

The great poet Kavi Karṇapūra has composed a verse which illustrates the intensity of the mutual love between Rādhā and Kṛṣṇa. Kṛṣṇa affectionately and amusingly addresses Rādhā,

To say "I am your love, and you are mine,"
Is but unworthy chatter I opine;
"You are my life, I yours," this to maintain,
Is verily mere idle prating vain;
It is inappropriate to attest
One is possessor, the other possessed;
The pronouns, O Rādhā, "you" and "me," thus,
Are improper in reference to us.[18]

The author elaborates the description of Lalitā and Viśākhā in the *Vraja-vilāsa-stava*, thus,

[18]Kavi Karṇapūra, *Alaṅkāra-kaustubha*, 5.34.

Surcharged with intense bliss and haughty pride,
In whom her friends intimately confide;
More dear than life to the amorous pair,
She prepares for their rendezvous with care,
She teaches her friend how to maintain pride,
And does always in their presence abide.
I bow down to Lalitā and prostrate,
May she make me her own associate.

With charming affection always disposed,
Where the couple's confidence is reposed,
She always acts for Vraja's sovereign pair,
With discourses and fond attentive care;
The dulcet singing of her voice when heard,
Rebukes the warbling of the Pika bird;
May Viśākhā, kind and compassionate,
Take me as her pupil initiate.[19]

Rādhākuṇḍa and Mount Govardhana,

With all due reverence and pious care,
On his lowered head, Govardhan doth bear,
A charming lake known by Ariṣṭha's name,
Which from Bakāri's kick a lake became.
Thus he more dear than Śiva, as beseems,
Who bears upon his head the Gaṅgā's streams.
A million times more sanctifying still,
Is Rādhā's lake, which like a precious jewel,
The high grace of Murajit does confer
Upon the devout praising worshiper.
Who is that pious one who would not take
Refuge at Govardhan and dwelling make?[20]

Verse Ten: Rādhā's Excellence

The author delineates, in the pride of conscious superiority, the superlative and supernal excellence of Rādhā, in comparison to other

[19]Raghunātha Dāsa, *Vraja-vilāsa-stava*, 29-30.
[20]Raghunātha Dāsa, *Govardhanāśraya-daśaka*, 5.

renowned goddesses.

रतिं गौरीलीले अपि तपति सौन्दर्यकिरणैः
शचीलक्ष्मीसत्याः परिभवति सौभाग्यबलनैः ।
वशीकारैश्चन्द्रावलीमुखनवीनव्रजसतीः
क्षिपत्याराद्या तां हरिदयितराधां भज मनः ॥ १० ॥

ratiṃ gaurīlīle api tapati saundaryakiraṇaiḥ
śacīlakṣmīsatyāḥ paribhavati saubhāgyabalanaiḥ |
vaśīkāraiścandrāvalīmukhanavīnavrajasatīḥ
kṣipatyārādyā tāṃ haridayitarādhāṃ bhaja manaḥ || 10 ||

Hari's beloved Rādhikā adore,
O mind, in contemplation, I implore.
Her charming beauty shines with dazzling rays;
Rati, Gaurī, Līlā, with envy blaze;
The power of her fortune puts to shame,
Śacī, Lakṣmī, Satyā, of worthy fame;
And even Vraja's cowherd damosels,
Among whom fair Candrāvalī excels,
Are cast aside by her superior grace,
And all their pride of beauty hers does efface.

Verse Eleven: The Five Nectars

In the final teaching of *Manaḥ-śikṣā*, the author supplies an enumeration of the devout disciplines and practices prescribed, as an adherent of Śrī Rūpa, his guide and preceptor.

समं श्रीरूपेण स्मरविवशराधागिरिभृतो-
र्व्रजे साक्षात्सेवालभनविधये तद्गणयुजोः ।
तदिज्याख्याध्यानश्रवणनतिपञ्चामृतमिदम्
धयन्नीत्या गोवर्धनमनुदिनं त्वं भज मनः ॥ ११ ॥

samaṃ śrīrūpeṇa smaravivaśarādhāgiribhṛto-

rvraje sāksātsevālabhanavidhaye tadgaṇayujoḥ |
tadijyākhyādhyānaśravaṇanatipañcāmṛtamidam
dhayannītyā govardhanamanudinaṃ tvaṃ bhaja manaḥ || 11||

O mind, as Śrī Rūpa's associate,
Imbibe the five nectars immaculate:
To worship Govardhan and sing his name,
To bow and meditate and hear his fame.
The drinking of these five nectars each day,
While at mount Govardhan you make your stay,
Is verily the direct means to gain
Service of him who lifted a mountain,
And of Radha, (while engrossed in sweet amour,
Surrounded by companions in the bower).

See *Upadeśāmṛta*, text 8 and notes for an examination of devotional disciplines.

Verse Twelve: The Singer's Benefit

The divine author concludes by offering a customary benediction to the reciter of *Manaḥ-śikṣā*.

मनःशिक्षादैकादशकवरमेतन्मधुरया
गिरा गायत्युच्चैः समधिगतसर्वार्थततिर्यः ।
सयूथः श्रीरूपानुग इह भवन् गोकुलवने
जनो राधाकृष्णातुलभजनरत्नं स लभते ॥ १२ ॥

manaḥśikṣādaikādaśakavarametanmadhurayā
girā gāyatyuccaiḥ samadhigatasarvārthatatiryaḥ |
sayūthaḥ śrīrūpānuga iha bhavan gokulavane
jano rādhākṛṣṇātulabhajanaratnaṃ sa labhate || 12 ||

Whoever these eleven stanzas sings,
With a sweet voice which from a pure heart springs,
That take the form of lessons to the mind,

All their desires accomplished sure will find.
And—dwelling here in Gokul's shady wood,
And emulating Rūpa in his mood,
And keeping society with the good—
The rarest gem of worship they'll receive,
(And Rādhā-Kṛṣṇa's boundless love achieve).

Kṛṣṇa playing his flute

(Freer Gallery: Sri Krsna with the flute, FS-6557_05, Public Domain)

Appendix 1: The Life of Raghunātha Dāsa Gosvāmin

Here is a brief account to glorify
The life and acts of Śrī Dāsa Gosāi.
For fuller knowledge I would recommend,
To each sympathetic reader and friend,
Perusing chapter six with minute care,
In the Last Part, and ye will find it there;
In close study of that chapter engage
In *Caitanya-caritamṛta*'s page!

All hail to Raghunāth who fled away,
And left his wealthy parents in dismay,
Although they'd kept him guarded and confined,
The fetters of worldliness could not bind.
For heavenly opulence he had no care,
And though his wife was like an angel fair,
He left her and his great prosperity,
The moon-like face of Caitanya to see.
He left his family in sore distress,
Being no more than nineteen years, I guess.
He first to Pāṇihāṭi village went,
And at the feet of Nitāi humbly bent,
On Nitāi's order held a festive treat,
Of chipped rice, yogurt, and bananas sweet;

And by lord Nityānanda's favour won
The mercy of chaste Śaci's noble son;
He thence proceeded to the holy place
Of Jagannāth, eager to gain his grace,
And meeting there his lord Gaurāṅga Rāy,
He fell prostrate and could do naught but cry.
He then was handed over to the care
Of Dāmodar, who did to him declare,
The mysteries of worship in the mind,
Leaving all pride and power of wealth behind.
From that day forth he was well known to fame,
As the Raghunāth of Svarūp by name.
His fastings and his practices austere,
'Tis said, were carved in stone, and most severe.
Thus he, dispassionate, there did remain,
And stern rules of a recluse did maintain.
And Gaurachandra gave to him his own
Necklace of *guñja* beads, and a small stone
From Govardhan, which were to him most dear,
Which, when meditating, he used to wear.
But when Gaura withdrew himself and left
This world, he felt despondent and bereft.

Anon he to Vṛndāvan did repair,
And dwelt with Rūpa and Sanātan there;
They urged him, in his grief and mental strife,
With fond affection, not to take his life;
For, since the time when Gaura left this world,
He was into deep melancholy hurled;
But thence to lovely Rādhā-kuṇḍ he came,
Immersed in nectar of the holy name.
Thus the great Dās Goswami dwelt for years
By Rādhā-kuṇḍ, augmenting it with tears,
In flights of rapture many a verse composed,
And Rādhā's glory to the world exposed.
In such texts as *A Collection of Prayers*,
Or that which the name of *Pearl Story* bears;
And other works, eloquent and refined,
Such as the famous *Teachings to the Mind*;

The wondrous story of the toll booth game,
Dāna-keli-cintāmaṇi by name.
And if it be some titles here are missed,
Vide the *Stavāvalī* for the list.

by Madanmohandas

Appendix 2: Eight Verses on Śrī Caitanya (Śrīcaitanyāṣṭaka)

Verse One: Kṛṣṇa's Descent as Caitanya

हरिर्दृष्ट्वा गोष्ठे मुकुरगतमात्मानमतुलं
स्वमाधुर्यं राधाप्रियतरसखीवाप्तुमभितः ।
अहो गौडे जातः प्रभुरपरगौरैकतनुभाक्
शचीसूनुः किं मे नयनशरणीं यास्यति पुनः ॥१॥

harirdṛṣṭvā goṣṭhe mukuragatamātmānamatulaṃ
svamādhuryaṃ rādhāpriyatarasakhīvāptumabhitaḥ |
aho gauḍe jātaḥ prabhuraparagauraikatanubhāk
śacīsūnuḥ kiṃ me nayanaśaraṇīṃ yāsyati punaḥ ||1||

After seeing himself in a
mirror in his cowherd village,
Lord Hari, to enjoy fully
his own unequaled sweetness—as does
Rādhā, his dearest beloved—
took birth, imagine, in Bengal,
in another golden body.
O will Śacī's son come again
into the path of my vision? (1)

Verse Two: Caitanya's Companions

पुरीदेवस्यान्तःप्रणयमधुनि स्नानमधुरो
मुहुर्गोविन्दोद्यद्विशदपरिचर्यार्चितपदः ।
स्वरूपस्य प्राणार्बुदकमलनीराजितमुखः
शचीसूनुः किं मे नयनशरणीं यास्यति पुनः ॥२॥

purīdevasyāntaḥpraṇayamadhuni snānamadhuro
muhurgovindodyadviśadaparicaryārcitapadaḥ |
svarūpasya prāṇārbudakamalanīrājitamukhaḥ
śacīsūnuḥ kiṃ me nayanaśaraṇīṃ yāsyati punaḥ ||2||

His sweetness bathed in the honey of
Īśvarapurī's[1] inner love,
his feet constantly honored by
Govinda's[2] pure, diligent
service, his face luminated
by the lotuses of Svarūpa's[3]
one hundred million vital breaths—
O will Śacī's son come again
into the path of my vision? (2)

Verse Three: Caitanya's Appearance

दधानः कौपीनं तदुपरि बहिर्वस्त्रमरुणं
प्रकाण्डो हेमाद्रिद्युतिभिरभितः सेविततनुः ।
मुदा गायन्नुच्चैर्निजमधुरनामावलिमसौ
शचीसूनुः किं मे नयनशरणीं यास्यति पुनः ॥३॥

dadhānaḥ kaupīnaṃ tadupari bahirvastramaruṇaṃ
prakāṇḍo hemādridyutibhirabhitaḥ sevitatanuḥ|
mudā gāyannuccairnijamadhuranāmāvalimasau
śacīsūnuḥ kiṃ me nayanaśaraṇīṃ yāsyati punaḥ||3||

---

[1]Caitanya's initiating guru.
[2]Caitanya's personal servant.
[3]Caitanya's renunciant friend, member of his inner circle, and Raghunātha Dāsa's guide.

Wearing a loincloth and above
that an outer cloth of saffron,
his superb body suffused with
the colors of a golden mountain,
singing loudly his own sweet names—
O will Śacī's son come again
into the path of my vision? (3)

Verse Four: Bhakti Revealed

अनावेद्यां पूर्वैरपि मुनिगणैर्भक्तिनिपुणैः
श्रुतेर्गूढां प्रेमोज्ज्वलरसफलां भक्तिलतिकाम।
कृपालुस्तां गौडे प्रभुरतिकृपाभिः प्रकटयन्
शचीसूनुः किं मे नयनशरणीं यास्यति पुनः ॥४॥

anāvedyāṃ pūrvairapi munigaṇairbhaktinipuṇaiḥ
śrutergūḍhāṃ premojjvalarasaphalāṃ bhaktilatikām|
kṛpālustāṃ gauḍe prabhuratikṛpābhiḥ prakaṭayan
śacīsūnuḥ kiṃ me nayanaśaraṇīṃ yāsyati punaḥ||4||

Even though it was unmentioned
by previous sages who were
experts in *bhakti*, and hidden
in the Vedas, the *bhakti* vine,
whose fruit is the blazing rapture
of love, was revealed by the Lord
with great compassion in Bengal.
O will Śacī's son come again
into the path of my vision? (4)

Verse Five: Caitanya's Main Teaching

निजत्वे गौडीयान् जगति परिगृह्य प्रभुरिमान्
हरे कृष्णेत्येवं गणनविधिना कीर्तयत भोः।
इति प्रायां शिक्षां चरणमधुपेभ्यः परिदिशन्
शचीसूनुः किं मे नयन-शरणीं यास्यति पुनः ॥५॥

nijatve gauḍīyān jagati parigṛhya prabhurimān
hare kṛṣṇetyevaṃ gaṇanavidhinā kīrtayata bhoḥ|
iti prāyāṃ śikṣāṃ caraṇamadhupebhyaḥ paridiśan
śacīsūnuḥ kiṃ me nayana-śaraṇīṃ yāsyati punaḥ ||5||

The Lord, accepting these Bengalis
as his own in the world, has given
the honey bees at his feet
their most important instruction:
"Hey! Counting, sing 'Hare Kṛṣṇa'"—
O will Śacī's son come again
into the path of my vision? (5)

Verse Six: Caitanya in Jagannātha's Temple

पुरः पश्यन्नीलाचलपतिमुरुप्रेमनिवहैः
क्षरन्नेत्राम्भोभिः स्नपितनिजदीर्घोज्ज्वलतनुः।
सदा तिष्ठन् देशे प्रणयिगरुडस्तम्भचरमे
शचीसूनुः किं मे नयन-शरणीं यास्यति पुनः ॥ ६ ॥

puraḥ paśyannīlācalapatimurupremanivahaiḥ
kṣarannetrāmbhobhiḥ snapitanijadīrghojjvalatanuḥ|
sadā tiṣṭhan deśe praṇayigaruḍastambhacarame
śacīsūnuḥ kiṃ me nayana-śaraṇīṃ yāsyati punaḥ||6||

Viewing before him the Lord of
the Blue Mountain,[4] his tall, glowing
body awash with tears flowing
from his eyes because of vast love—
always standing in place behind
dearly loved Garuḍa's column—
O will Śacī's son come again
into the path of my vision? (6)

[4]Lord of the Blue Mountain (Nīlācalapati) refers to Lord Jagannātha, the main sacred image in the temple at Jagannātha Purī.

Verse Seven: Caitanya's Ecstatic Dance

मुदा दन्तैर्दष्ट्वा द्युतिविजितबन्धूकमधरं
करं कृत्वा वामं कटिनिहितमन्यं परिलसन।
समुत्थाप्य प्रेम्णागणितपुलको नृत्यकुतुकी
शचीसूनुः किं मे नयनशरणीं यास्यति पुनः ॥७॥

mudā dantairdaṣṭvā dyutivijitabandhūkamadharaṃ
karaṃ kṛtvā vāmaṃ kaṭinihitamanyaṃ parilasan|
samutthāpya premṇāgaṇitapulako nṛtyakutukī
śacīsūnuḥ kiṃ me nayanaśaraṇīṃ yāsyati punaḥ||7||

That joyful, arduous dancer,
bit with his teeth his lower lip,
the color of which bests the red
bandhūka flowers. On his hip
he placed his left hand and, as
he danced to and fro, his other hand
he raised high; from love, the countless
hairs on his body stood erect—
O will Śacī's son come again
into the path of my vision? (7)

Verse Eight: Caitanya's Love-in-Separation

सरित्तीरारामे विरहविधुरो गोकुलविधो-
र्नदीमन्यां कुर्वन्नयनजलधाराविततिभिः।
मुहुर्मूर्च्छां गच्छन्मृतकमिव विश्वं विरचयन्
शचीसूनुः किं मे नयनशरणीं यास्यति पुनः ॥८॥

sarittīrārāme virahavidhuro gokulavidho-
rnadīmanyāṃ kurvannayanajaladhārāvitatibhiḥ|
muhurmūrcchāṃ gacchanmṛtakamiva viśvaṃ viracayan
śacīsūnuḥ kiṃ me nayanaśaraṇīṃ yāsyati punaḥ||8||

He, in a grove on a river's

bank, distressed by separation
from the Moon of Gokula, made
another river from the tears
streaming from his eyes; and fainting
again and again he transmuted
the living world into a corpse.
O will Śacī's son come again
into the path of my vision? (8)

Verse Nine: The Effect of Reciting this Poem

शचीसूनोरस्याष्टकमिदमभीष्टं विरचयत्
सदा दैन्योद्रेकादतिविशदबुद्धिः पठति यः।
प्रकामं चैतन्यः प्रभुरतिकृपावेशविवशः
पृथुप्रेमाम्भोधौ प्रथितरसदे मज्जयति तम् ॥९॥

śacīsūnorasyāṣṭakamidamabhīṣṭaṃ viracayat
sadā dainyodrekādativiśadabuddhiḥ paṭhati yaḥ|
prakāmaṃ caitanyaḥ prabhuratikṛpāveśavivaśaḥ
pṛthupremāmbhodhau prathitarasade majjayati tam||9||

One who, with great humility
and with a pristine intellect,
always recites this fine octet,
focused on the Son of Śacī,
which makes what's wished for come to be—
Lord Caitanya, rendered helpless,
being possessed by great kindness,
submerges that reciter in
an ocean of vast selfless love
where celebrated *rasa*'s found. (9)

इति श्रीरघुनाथदासगोस्वामिविरचितस्तवावल्यां श्रीशचीसूनवष्टकं सम्पूर्णम।

Thus ends, the "Octet of Verses on the Son of Śacī (Śrī Caitanya)" in the *Garland of Praises* written by Śrī Raghunātha Dāsa Gosvāmin.

Appendix 3: Wishing Tree of Praise of Śrī Gaurāṅga (Śrīgaurāṅgastavakalpa-taru)

Verse One: Caitanya's Beauty

गतिं दृष्ट्वा यस्य प्रमदगजवर्ये'खिलजना
मुखं च श्रीचन्द्रोपरि दधति थूत्कारनिवहम् ।
स्वकान्त्या यः स्वर्णाचलमधरयच्छीधु च वच-
स्तरङ्गैर्गौराङ्गो हृदय उदयन् मां मदयति ॥ १ ॥

gatiṃ dṛṣṭvā yasya pramadagajavarye'khilajanā
mukhaṃ ca śrīcandropari dadhati thūtkāranivaham |
svakāntyā yaḥ svarṇācalamadharayacchīdhu ca vaca-
staraṅgairgaurāṅgo hṛdaya udayan māṃ madayati ||1||

Seeing his manner of walking and his face, people spit dismissively on the finest of drunken elephants, and on the full moon. By his physical glow he makes a mountain of gold wish to return to the womb. On the

waves of his sweet speech, Gaurāṅga,
rising in my heart, delights me. (1)

Verse Two: Caitanya's Ecstatic Symptons

अलङ्कृत्यात्मानं नवविविधरत्नैरिव वल-
द्विवर्णत्वस्तम्भास्फुटवचनकम्पाश्रुपुलकैः ।
हसन् स्विद्यन्नृत्यन् शितिगिरिपतेर्निर्भरमुदे
पुरः श्रीगौराङ्गो हृदय उदयन् मां मदयति ॥२॥

alaṅkṛtyātmānaṃ navavividharatnairiva vala-
dvivarṇatvastambhāsphuṭavacanakampāśrupulakaiḥ |
hasan svidyannṛtyan śitigiripaternirbharamude
puraḥ śrīgaurāṅgo hṛdaya udayan māṃ madayati ||2||

Decorating[1] himself, as if
with various new kinds of gems—
paleness, stupor, stammering,
shivering, tears, and goose bumps,
laughing, sweating, dancing before
the Lord of the Blue Mountain[2]—
in immense joy Śrī Gaurāṅga
rising in my heart delights me. (2)

Verse Three: Caitanya's Ecstatic Dance

रसोल्लासैस्तिर्यग्गतिभिरभितो वारिभिरलं
दृशोः सिञ्चन् लोकानरुणजलयन्त्रत्वमितयोः ।
मुदा दन्तैर्दष्ट्वा मधुरमधरं कम्पचलितै-
र्नटन् श्रीगौराङ्गो हृदय उदयन् मां मदयति ॥३॥

[1]The commentator, Baṅgeśvara Vidyābhūṣaṇa, provides context for the appearance of these ecstatic symptoms in Caitanya, "Suddenly, while Rādhā is feeling love-in-separation from Kṛṣṇa because Kṛṣṇa has gone to Mathurā, Kṛṣṇa appears to her and her heart is overwhelmed with love." Joy simultaneously manifests in Caitanya.

[2]Śitigiripati, Lord of the Blue Mountain, is another name for the Jagannātha deity in Purī.

rasollāsaistiryaggatibhirabhito vāribhiralaṃ
dṛśoḥ siñcan lokānaruṇajalayantratvamitayoḥ |
mudā dantairdaṣṭvā madhuramadharaṃ kampacalitai-
rnaṭan śrīgaurāṅgo hṛdaya udayan māṃ madayati ||3||

Staggering from side to side in
rasa's[3] delight,[4] his eyes, sprinkling
enough water to moisten the worlds,
turn into red water wheels, and,
biting in joy his sweet lower lip
with teeth made to chatter by tremors
as he dances, Śrī Gaurāṅga
rising in my heart delights me. (3)

Verse Four: Caitanya's Love-in-Separation

क्वचिन्मिश्रावासे व्रजपतिसुतस्योरुविरहात्
श्लथच्छ्रीसन्धित्वाद्दधदधिकदैर्घ्यं भुजपदोः ।
लुठन् भूमौ काक्वा विकलविकलं गद्गदवचा
रुदन् श्रीगौराङ्गो हृदय उदयन् मां मदयति ॥४॥

kvacinmiśrāvāse vrajapatisutasyoruvirahāt
ślathacchrīsandhitvāddadhadadhikadairghyaṃ bhujapadoḥ |
luṭhan bhūmau kākvā vikalavikalaṃ gadgadavacā
rudan śrīgaurāṅgo hṛdaya udayan māṃ madayati ||4||

Sometimes at Kāśīmiśra's house,
feeling intense separation[5]

[3]Sacred rapture (*bhakti-rasa*).

[4]The commentator again supplies a context for this delight of Caitanya's: "Thinking that Kṛṣṇa, having had a change of heart, has returned from Mathurā, Rādhā says to him, 'O Crown Jewel of Rasa Lovers, Lord of My Life! Where did you go leaving me behind helpless? So cruel you are! Don't forget poor me again even in dream!'" And in explanation of Caitanya's dancing, the commentator says, "Kṛṣṇa says, 'I will never again leave you, who are dearer than my life, and go anywhere else.' Thinking this, Caitanya begins to dance in joy."

[5]Commentator: "No longer seeing Kṛṣṇa any more, Rādhā's heart again becomes unsettled with separation. This condition is described in Caitanya in the next six verses."

from Kṛṣṇa, the Lord of Vraja,
he wept, arms and legs becoming
lengthened from the loosening of
his joints, and he rolled on the ground
with garbled, stammering, broken-
pitched speech—O Śrī Gaurāṅga
rising in my heart delights me. (4)

Verse Five: Caitanya's Love-in-Separation (2)

अनुद्घाट्य द्वारत्रयमुरु च भित्तित्रयमहो
विलङ्घ्योच्चैः कालिङ्गिकसुरभिमध्ये निपतितः ।
तनूद्यत्सङ्कोचात् कमठ इव कृष्णोरुविरहाद्
विराजन् गौराङ्गो हृदय उदयन् मां मदयति ॥५॥

anudghāṭya dvāratrayamuru ca bhittitrayamaho
vilaṅghyoccaiḥ kāliṅgikasurabhimadhye nipatitaḥ |
tanūdyatsaṅkocāt kamaṭha iva kṛṣṇoruvirahād
virājan gaurāṅgo hṛdaya udayan māṃ madayati ||5||

Without opening three large doors and
somehow crossing over three high walls,
he fell amidst Orissan cows.
His body rose and contracted
like a turtle's because he felt
great separation from Kṛṣṇa.
Appearing so—Śrī Gaurāṅga
rising in my heart delights me. (5)

Verse Six: Caitanya Longs For Vraja

स्वकीयस्य प्राणार्बुदसदृशगोष्ठस्य विरहात्
प्रलापानुन्मादात्सततमति कुर्वन् विकलधीः ।
दधद्भित्तौ शश्वद्वदनविधुघर्षेण रुधिरं
क्षातोत्थं गौराङ्गो हृदय उदयन् मां मदयति ॥६॥

svakīyasya prāṇārbudasadṛśagoṣṭhasya virahāt
pralāpānunmādātsatatamati kurvan vikaladhīḥ |
dadhadbhittau śaśvadvadanavidhugharṣeṇa rudhiraṃ
kṣātotthaṃ gaurāṅgo hṛdaya udayan māṃ madayati ||6||

Missing his own cowherd town,
dearer to him than one
hundred million breaths of life,
he uttered insane word salads non-stop,
his mind fully agitated.
His blood rising from wounds made by
rubbing his moon face repeatedly
against a [rough] wall—Śrī Gaurāṅga
rising in my heart delights me. (6)

Verse Seven: Caitanya Searches for Kṛṣṇa

क्व मे कान्तः कृष्णस्त्वरितमिह तं लोकय सखे
त्वमेवेति द्वाराधिपमभिवदन्नुन्मद इव ।
द्रुतं गच्छ द्रष्टुं प्रियमिति तदुक्तेन धृततद्-
भुजान्तर्गौराङ्गो हृदय उदयन् मां मदयति ॥७॥

kva me kāntaḥ kṛṣṇastvaritamiha taṃ lokaya sakhe
tvameveti dvārādhipamabhivadannunmada iva |
drutaṃ gaccha draṣṭuṃ priyamiti taduktena dhṛtatad-
bhujāntargaurāṅgo hṛdaya udayan māṃ madayati ||7||

"My lover Kṛṣṇa, where is he?
Quickly, show him to me here, O friend,"
Caitanya addressed the gate's guard[6]
like a madman. He, with the words,
"Go speedily to see your dear,"
took Caitanya's hand. Gaurāṅga
rising in my heart delights me. (7)

[6]A guard at the gate of the Jagannātha temple in Purī.

Verse Eight: Caitanya Spots Govardhana

समीपे नीलाद्रेश्चटकगिरिराजस्य कलनाद्
अये गोष्ठे गोवर्धनगिरिपतिं लोकितुम् इतः ।
व्रजन्नस्मीत्युक्त्वा प्रमद इव धावन्नवधृतो
गणैः स्वैर्गौराङ्गो हृदय उदयन् मां मदयति ॥८॥

samīpe nīlādreścaṭakagirirājasya kalanād
aye goṣṭhe govardhanagiripatiṃ lokitum itaḥ |
vrajannasmītyuktvā pramada iva dhāvannavadhṛto
gaṇaiḥ svairgaurāṅgo hṛdaya udayan māṃ madayati ||8||

Spotting the king of hills, Sparrow,
near Blue Mountain, he said "Oy! I am
going from here to Vraja to see
the king of hills Govardhana,"
and, so resolved, began running
like a madman along with
his followers— Gaurāṅga
rising in my heart delights me, (8)

Verse Nine: Caitanya Sings Kṛṣṇa's Names

अलं दोलाखेलामहसि वरतन्मण्डपतले
स्वरूपेण स्वेनापरनिजगणेनापि मिलितः ।
स्वयं कुर्वन्नाम्नाम् अतिमधुरगानं मुरभिदः
सरङ्गो गौराङ्गो हृदय उदयन् मां मदयति ॥९॥

alaṃ dolākhelāmahasi varatanmaṇḍapatale
svarūpeṇa svenāparanijagaṇenāpi militaḥ |
svayaṃ kurvannāmnām atimadhuragānaṃ murabhidaḥ
saraṅgo gaurāṅgo hṛdaya udayan māṃ madayati ||9||

At the beautiful festival
celebrating the Swing Līlā,
on the floor of the fine pavilion,
together with Svarūpa and
others of his dear companions,

he himself sang very sweet songs
using the names of Mura's Splitter [Kṛṣṇa],
his songs enhanced by acting—Gaurāṅga
rising in my heart delights me. (9)

Verse Ten: Caitanya Acts Like Kṛṣṇa

दयां यो गोविन्दे गरुड इव लक्ष्मीपतिरलं
पुरीदेवे भक्तिं य इव गुरुवर्ये यदुवरः ।
स्वरूपे यः स्नेहं गिरिधर इव श्रीलसुबले
विधत्ते गौराङ्गो हृदय उदयन् मां मदयति ॥१०॥

dayāṃ yo govinde garuḍa iva lakṣmīpatiralaṃ
purīdeve bhaktiṃ ya iva guruvarye yaduvaraḥ |
svarūpe yaḥ snehaṃ giridhara iva śrīlasubale
vidhatte gaurāṅgo hṛdaya udayan māṃ madayati ||10||

He showed compassion to Govinda[7]
like the Lord of Lakṣmī did
to Garuḍa; *bhakti* to Lord
Purī[8] like the Best of Yadus[9]
did to his guru;[10] affection
to Svarūpa[11] like the Lifter
of the Mountain[12] did
to Śrī Subala[13]—Gaurāṅga
rising in my heart delights me. (10)

[7] Śrī Caitanya's personal servant.
[8] Īśvara Purī.
[9] Kṛṣṇa.
[10] Sāndīpani Muni.
[11] Svarūpa Dāmodara.
[12] Kṛṣṇa.
[13] One of Kṛṣṇa's close friends.

Verse Eleven: Caitanya Saves Raghunātha Dāsa

महासम्पद्दावादपि पतितमुद्धृत्य कृपया
स्वरूपे यः स्वीये कुजनमपि मां न्यस्य मुदितः ।
उरोगुञ्जाहारं प्रियमपि च गोवर्धनशिलां
ददौ मे गौराङ्गो हृदय उदयन् मां मदयति ॥११॥

mahāsampaddāvādapi patitamuddhṛtya kṛpayā
svarūpe yaḥ svīye kujanamapi māṃ nyasya muditaḥ |
uroguñjāhāraṃ priyamapi ca govardhanaśilāṃ
dadau me gaurāṅgo hṛdaya udayan māṃ madayati ||11||

Out of compassion, he, lifted
me up who had fallen because
of great prosperity and wife,
and, though I was a bad person,
placed me happily with his own
Svarūpa, gave me the *guñjā-*
necklace from his chest,
though it was dear to him, and his
Govardhana stone—Gaurāṅga
rising in my heart delights me. (11)

Verse Twelve: Gaining the Fruit of the Divine Tree

इति श्रीगौराङ्गोद्गतविविधसद्भावकुसुम-
प्रभाभ्राजत्पद्यावलिललितशाखं सुरतरुम् ।
मुहुर्यो’तिश्रद्धौषधिवरबलत्पाठसलिलै-
रलं सिञ्चेद्विन्देत् सरसगुरुतल्लोकनफलम् ॥१२॥

iti śrīgaurāṅgodgatavividhasadbhāvakusuma-
prabhābhrājatpadyāvalilalitaśākhaṃ suratarum |
muhuryo'tiśraddhauṣadhivarabalatpāṭhasalilai-
ralaṃ siñcedvindet sarasagurutallokanaphalam ||12||

One who sprinkles repeatedly,

with the waters of recitation,
empowered by the best
medicinal herb, [which is] great faith,
this wish-fulfilling tree [this poem] whose
graceful branches are songs aglow
with the luster of the blossoms
of the many pure feelings
which arose in Śrī Gaurāṅga,
will gain as reward the merciful
gaze of a rasa-filled guru. (12)

इति श्रीमद्रघुनाथदासगोस्वामिविरचितस्तवावल्यां श्रीगौराङ्गस्तवकल्पतरुः समाप्तः ।

iti śrīmadraghunāthadāsagosvāmiviracitastavāvalyāṃ śrīgaurāṅgastava-kalpataruḥ samāptaḥ |

Thus ends the "Wishing Tree of Praise of Śrī Gaurāṅga" in the *Garland of Praises* written by Śrī Raghunātha Dāsa Gosvāmin.

www.ingramcontent.com/pod-product-compliance
Lightning Source LLC
Chambersburg PA
CBHW052112110526
44592CB00013B/1577
* 9 7 8 1 9 5 2 2 3 2 5 2 7 *